# SEASONS
*Reflections on Changes Throughout Life*
## KATHERINE WALDEN

Copyright © 2015 Katherine Walden

All rights reserved.

Revised 2015

ISBN:
0993857205
9780993857201

All rights reserved to Katherine Walden and I Lift My Eyes Ministries. No portion of this book may be stored electronically, transmitted, copied, reproduced or reprinted for commercial gain or profit without prior written permission by Katherine Walden. Contact information is listed below.

Home groups, Bible study groups and any online entities may use short quotes or an occasional devotional as long as proper attribution is made.

I Lift My Eyes Ministries
c/o Harvest Vineyard Christian Fellowship
11602 - 40 Street NW
Edmonton, AB
Canada
T5W 2K6

An online contact form is available on [katherinewalden.com](katherinewalden.com)

All Bible references are taken from the English Standard Version unless otherwise noted.

English Standard Version (ESV)
The Holy Bible, English Standard Version Copyright © 2001 by Crossway Bibles, a division of Good News Publishers.

The Message (MSG)
Copyright © 1993, 1994, 1995, 1996, 2000, 2001, 2002 by Eugene H. Peterson

Some names and locations have been changed to protect the privacy of those concerned.

# SEASONS

## Table of Contents

| | |
|---|---|
| Introduction | 01 |
| New Life in the New Year | 03 |
| One Way to Break My Eyeglass Habit | 07 |
| To Whom Are You Listening? | 10 |
| The Milestones of Maturity | 12 |
| His Paths are not Always Pleasant | 14 |
| Crawl Your Way Up | 17 |
| Now What Do We Do? | 21 |
| The Big Stick | 23 |
| The First Signs of Spring | 26 |
| Mutual Appreciation Society | 29 |
| In It For The Long Haul | 32 |
| On Them Has Light Shone | 34 |
| He's Not Dead Yet! | 39 |
| Inattentive Receiving | 41 |
| A Winter's Caress | 44 |
| Shirley, Goodness and Mercy | 46 |
| Laying Down Our Crowns | 50 |
| I Was Homesick | 52 |
| Give From What You've Been Given | 55 |
| Watching Them Soar | 57 |
| There Is Always the Promise of Daylight | 60 |
| The Living Is Easy | 63 |
| Taste and See That the Lord is Good | 65 |
| He Is the Air I Breathe | 68 |
| What's a Little Snow Going to Hurt? | 70 |
| Let a Fresh Breeze In! | 72 |
| Head for the Lifeboat | 75 |
| Go into Egypt | 77 |
| His Mirror Never Lies | 80 |
| Sow Gratitude | 83 |
| Do We Know Him? | 85 |
| What's Yours is Mine, What's Mine is Mine | 88 |
| Clear Your Closet | 90 |
| Everything Else Pales in Comparison | 92 |
| People Get Ready | 95 |

| | |
|---|---|
| Stirring Up a Hornet's Nest | 97 |
| God's Ambassadors | 100 |
| Can't Get a Word in Edgewise? | 102 |
| Getting Out of the Way | 105 |
| My Times Are in His Hands | 107 |
| Flee the Tyranny of Immediacy | 109 |
| When the World's All That It Should Be | 111 |
| Walking In Obedience | 113 |
| His Kindness Leads to Repentance | 118 |
| My God is Not Stone-Faced | 121 |
| The Promised Land is Occupied | 124 |
| Now That I Have Your Attention | 127 |
| Is It Time to Let Go of Your Night Light? | 130 |
| Free Fall | 133 |
| To Every Season… | 135 |
| The Fog Will Lift | 138 |
| I Told You Twice, Isn't That Enough? | 141 |
| The Storm Chasers | 144 |
| A Cup of Water in My Name | 146 |
| Don't Sweat the Small Stuff | 149 |
| The Field God Gives | 151 |
| A Thousand May Fall at Your Side | 153 |
| The Farmer's Gamble | 156 |
| Maintain Your Blessing | 159 |
| Give, No Matter What the Season! | 165 |
| Have You Checked Your Insurance Policy? | 167 |
| The Long and Winding Road | 170 |
| Our God Longs For Us | 172 |
| He Knows the Rest of Our Story | 176 |
| The Master's Touch | 179 |
| Come See What You Gave Me! | 181 |
| Serving in Assured Authority | 184 |
| So, What Do You Do? | 187 |
| Cultivating Kindness | 190 |
| Relishing Obscurity | 193 |
| God is Good, Always! | 195 |
| Trying to Find a Way Through? | 197 |
| The Yellow Bowl Blessing | 199 |

| | |
|---|---|
| I Cannot be at Peace Standing Still | 202 |
| No Small Thing | 204 |
| We Bring Pleasure to God's Heart | 207 |
| God's Remedy for Blue Mondays | 209 |
| No Matter How Hard I Try… | 212 |
| Just Do It | 214 |
| Don't Let Your Light Diminish | 217 |
| Stones of Remembrance | 220 |
| Peace! Be Still! | 222 |
| I Don't Have to Always Know | 225 |
| Use Your Tools Wisely | 227 |
| I'm Just Not That Strong | 231 |
| God of All Comfort | 233 |
| The Wise Remain Students | 237 |
| Blessed Assurance | 239 |
| Worship With No Agenda | 241 |
| My Prayer For You | 243 |
| About the Author | 244 |
| Special Thanks | 245 |

*I dedicate this book to all those who wonder if their winter will ever end. May this book bring you hope. Spring is on the horizon!*

# INTRODUCTION

When a child, I often heard my mother say, "I can't believe how this week, this month, this year has flown by."

From an eight-year-old perspective, time seemed to crawl at a snail's pace, especially if I was awaiting the next great event marked on the big calendar on our kitchen wall. A sleep-over in February, my birthday in April, the end of school in June, a camping trip in August, Halloween in October and Christmas in December; they seemed to take forever to arrive.

And yet, even at such a young age, I understood the elasticity of time. The street lamps on my block turned on much too early, especially if I was enjoying a game of hide-and-seek. I knew once those lights glowed, all the mothers of the neighbourhood would be on their front steps calling their children home. An afternoon passed like a minute when it was spent at the neighbourhood swimming pool. Mind you, an afternoon passed like a month when it was spent sitting quietly beside my parents as they entertained distant relatives who wanted to see me but didn't necessarily want to hear me.

In the process of compiling this book, I sorted through hundreds of devotions I have written over the past 20 years, many of which are based on life experiences. Some go as far back as my childhood and my teen years while others were written about experiences I had while in missions. Many of the devotions I will share with you were written in times of great joy or intense sorrow. However, most were written as I traipsed through the mundane experiences of everyday life.

As I read through each devotion, I echo my mother's lament, "My, how time flies!" Nevertheless, I continue to experience the elasticity of time. What once appeared to be long, hard seasons of all-consuming pain and adversity are now only faint memories. Simple, yet timely, acts of compassion shown towards me more than 30 years ago continue to impact me today.

Seasons. We all go through them, no matter where we live on this planet. Winter, spring, summer and autumn. Times of loss and times of gain, times of joy and times of pain. Times of plenty and times of lack, times of growth and times of rest.

Ecclesiastes 3:1 - *"There is a right time for everything, and everything on earth will happen at the right time."*

## New Life in the New Year

New Year's Eve found me on the highway with a group of friends, heading toward a cabin at Pigeon Lake, Alberta, about an hour outside my city. The wind began to blow earlier in the afternoon, sweeping the warming effects of El Nino away and returning us to chilly seasonal norms. Although none of us had been to the lake before, we had received clear directions. As seasoned winter travellers, we were confident we would reach our friend's cabin with no difficulty.

Worship music blared, and we sang along, enjoying each other's company and anticipating the fun that lay ahead. Unfortunately, we were enjoying ourselves so much that we did not realize we missed our turn-off until we were well past the highway junction. Our driver made the decision to stay on the same road, believing that it would eventually intersect the road we should have taken. My gut kept saying, "Turn back and ask for help!" but I didn't speak up. Finally, we came to the next town along the way and phoned our host. He confirmed that yes, we had missed our turn, and yes, the only turnoff was 15 miles behind us.

The wind changed directions, bringing with it a fine blowing snow. Our driver became a little nervous, and I began to pray, asking the Lord to clear our path and guide our way. The blowing snow made it difficult to see the highway, and the winds made it hard for the driver to keep the car in the right lane. We turned down the music as we prayed. After a harrowing trip, we arrived at the cabin, an hour late. As we pulled into the driveway, the storm died down. If we had not made the error in judgment, we would have missed the snow completely, but the Lord was faithful in protecting us even in our foolishness.

Our anxious hosts greeted us and ushered us into a cozy living room. When we settled around the fire, we introduced ourselves to another guest who had arrived earlier. Tony soon endeared himself to us with his wit and compassion, and we felt that we had made a great new friend. We shared a wonderful meal together, feasting on fellowship and great food. Prayer intermingled our conversation as we waited for a carload of friends who had not yet arrived. Once everyone had found their way to the cabin, we entertained ourselves by joyfully sharing what God was doing in our lives. Tony looked on with interest. As the evening progressed, it became evident that he was not a committed Christian.

Just before midnight, we gathered around the wood stove in the living room. Someone asked if we were going to watch the ball drop in Times Square. Someone else suggested that we bring in the New Year with prayer and worship. We put on some worship CDs and sang in the New Year. As the music played on, we entered into deep worship. People were dancing, singing, and quietly worshipping. I glanced at Tony and saw tears running down his cheeks. He was deeply touched.

We slowly became quiet in the stillness of the Lord's presence among us, and Tony went outside for a cigarette. When he returned, I asked if we could pray with him. He agreed, and we gathered around our friend. As we prayed, God made His love evident to Tony. He began to sob, and I could feel God's love saturating him. He met the God who made his heart as clean as the sparkling, white snow that continued to fall during the night. We continued to pray for each other, and when we finally went to bed, it was 4:30 a.m.

I asked Tony at breakfast how he felt, and he said it was the strangest and the most wonderful New Year's Eve he had ever spent. He laughed as he admitted that it was the first time in many years that he hadn't woken up with a hangover on New Year's Day. We had an impromptu worship time just before we all headed home to the city, and Tony felt God's touch again.

Tony came to our church for a few months before his life led him away from our city, but I have never forgotten him or the miracle of his new birth.

## ONE WAY TO BREAK MY EYEGLASS HABIT

Several years ago, I received a miracle through the combination of advanced technology and the skilled hands of a brilliant eye surgeon. With the implantation of permanent, corrective lenses along with cataract surgery, I was no longer extremely near-sighted, and I was able to pick any frame in any optician's shop. I no longer needed thick lenses because I no longer had severe astigmatism. As I was a little strapped for cash, I chose a discount optician shop, an option that was not available to me before surgery.

A couple of years later, my designer frames fell apart. As they were beyond repair, a visit to my optometrist was in order. Coincidentally, I was due for a check-up. I worried that I would need a stronger prescription. I was experiencing eye fatigue, especially when I was reading fine print.

After a series of tests and careful examination of my eyes, the optometrist cheerfully announced that my vision had not altered since my surgery. I was perplexed. Why was I having difficulties, then?

Before I could voice my concern, my usually jovial doctor became serious as he pushed his chair closer to me. In a firm tone, he gave me his orders. I was not to wear my new glasses outside of computer work and reading fine print. Through his phrasing and inflection, I surmised that he was only repeating what he had previously told me. From the murky confines of my memory, I heard the faint echoes of his prior orders.

The light went on. "Oh!"

He really meant what he said. I was only to wear my glasses when reading or working on my computer. I was in danger of weakening my eyes by allowing them to become dependent on something they no longer needed. My distance vision was fine, but I needed to train my eyes to focus on the distance.

His smile returned at my befuddled expression. "Don't worry, you just need to be educated in using your new prescription, and we need to find you more suitable lenses." The light dawned brighter. "Ah! My last pair weren't suitable?" Leading me to his outer office, he introduced me to an optician whose shop was next to his clinic. She specialized in fitting my unique prescription, and it turned out that she had undergone a similar surgery and understood my situation.

After carefully measuring my eyes and making necessary calculations, she spent quite a bit of time with me, pointing out the pros and cons of various frames and lens combinations. I quickly learned that I got what I paid for at the optical bargain store. Although I was free to choose just about any frame in the store, the frame would have to be modified to fit my slight astigmatism. With a wink, she informed me that if I tried to wear my new glasses for any purpose other than their original intent, I would be dizzy and disoriented. I laughingly replied, "Ah, that's one way to break my habit of wearing eyeglasses!"

However, I was used to hiding behind the thick-framed eyeglasses I had been wearing since the age of seven. I felt exposed and uncomfortable for several weeks until both my friends and I adapted to my new appearance.

As I reflected on my experience, I could see similarities in my spiritual life. How often do I look at my world through the lens of my past experiences and preconceived ideas? How often does presumption cause me to miss God's direction? How often do I try to hide my true self behind shaded glasses of self-protection? Why do I settle for second best when God has so much more He would like to give to me?

## *To Whom Are You Listening?*

Moses sent twelve mighty men as spies into the Promised Land. Ten men returned with a message that struck fear, despair, and resistance in the camp. Two men returned with a message of hope, exhortation, and encouragement. The children of Israel chose to listen to the message of fear. An entire generation bore the devastating consequences of their fear-based decision.

In our media-driven age, we are bombarded with dire warnings on a daily basis. Economic soothsayers pronounce doom and gloom on a weekly basis. At the faintest whisper of regional instability, headlines blast across the world that the end is near. Political camps carefully craft election campaigns, presenting the worse case scenario, then brazenly present their candidates as modern-day messiahs who will lead their nation out of the sure disaster caused by their rivals.

Fear makes a terrible advisor. It is the worst possible foundation on which to base life-altering decisions. Fear causes you to cave into wild speculations. Fear clouds your heart and mind and tempts you to give more credence to the voice of man than to the voice of God.

Jesus did not sugar-coat the challenges that lay ahead for His disciples. He painted a clear picture of the future, including persecution, trials, and death. Like Joshua, Jesus promised an assured victory as long as they remained faithful. He exhorted His twelve disciples not to be alarmed then challenged them to keep their hearts untroubled.

His challenge echoes with His followers today. We have a choice. Do we listen to His voice and live in the sure peace that He is our good and perfect Shepherd? Or do we listen to the myriad of fear-mongers, allowing ourselves to be tossed to and fro in the winds of controversy, rumours, and deliberate misinformation that come across our desks?

## The Milestones of Maturity

One of the joys of attending a church that meets in a school gym is the freedom it affords toddlers, giving them plenty of space to explore their world. Over the years, I've watched dozens of children take their individual explorations down our main aisle, all at the same breakneck speed. "Hurry up, I've got places to go, people to see!" Nothing seems to distract them, not even the tempting dance ribbons and scarves that whip just out of their reach.

Brass-lidded housings for volleyball net poles are conveniently placed near the centre aisle of our church. A mysterious gene implanted deep in the DNA of our toddlers seems to be triggered between their first birthday and 18-month milestone, drawing them to the mysterious housings.

Most adults and older children walk across the brass covers without giving them a second thought, but to a toddler, the brass covers are one of the seven wonders of their world. The discovery so enthralls them that they stop dead in their tracks and fall to their knees to peer in amazement at the covers. These young investigators refuse to budge until they poke and prod, making sure to examine their discovery thoroughly.

I take pride in each child who successfully reaches this developmental milestone. I consider it a visible sign that they are taking the tentative steps past infancy and into toddlerhood, joining the ranks of young explorers in our church family.

Christians are engrafted into Jesus' bloodline. We not only model ourselves after Christ, but we also carry Christ within us, and we are carried in Him. When we are grafted into Christ Jesus, His life-giving blood not only sustains us but it also begins a transformation within us, conforming us into His image. As we abide in Him, we no longer bear bitter fruit. As we draw people into His sweetness, they bear witness to our transformation. Let's live our lives so they reflect the genetic heritage we now bear. May the words of our lips, the path of our feet, and the touch of our hands signify to others that we now carry God's DNA.

Lord, we give You permission to prune from our lives anything that would stop us from growing in You. Our heart's desire is that we give You a reason to beam with pride as we grow into maturity through Your Son. May nothing deter us from reaching the milestones You have set before us.

## *His Paths are not Always Pleasant*

When I was a child, the one person with whom I felt most secure often led me to places I did not wish to go. I remember placing my trusting hand in my mother's soft grip and walking with her into the doctor's office. The mother who soothed me and nurtured me was the same mother who led me straight into the examining room, sat me on the table and rolled up my sleeve. She even allowed the mean, old doctor to poke me with a sharp needle! In my 4-year-old mind, I felt betrayed. How could she do such a thing? It just wasn't fair!

Then there was the physiotherapy she made me go through week after week. The painful stretching of weakened muscles, the fatiguing weights, and the exhaustion that followed after! All of it caused me to miss the fun of playing with the other kids on the block. What a hard taskmaster she was! Why did I have to work when everyone else got to play? She just wasn't fair.

I now see her wisdom and her kindness. I see that those nasty, sharp needles inoculated me from the same fate as a classmate's sister, who lost her life due to a severe case of the measles. Decades after the gruelling years of physiotherapy, I am still walking, albeit shakily. I developed muscle strength and tone that doctors said would have never been possible without exercise.

I can only assume that my mother did some internal wailing of her own as she held me still for my infant vaccines. More than likely, her heart ached as I spent weeks in a hospital and then underwent months in physical therapy as a ten-year-old. I am sure she would have rather watched me play tag with the other neighbourhood kids, yet she prodded me daily to do just one more repetition with weights and just five more minutes on the exercise bike. Because she loved me, she knew she would have to lead me places that cost me momentary suffering. She knew that momentary suffering was necessary for my highest good.

I am the daughter of the Heavenly Father who is in all ways perfect. The One who walks beside me along difficult paths asks me to trust Him. As I put my hand in His, I know that no amount of complaining on my part will cause Him to loosen His gentle grip. I know that any road on which He takes me will ultimately lead me toward His blessings.

Hebrews 12:11-13 - *For the moment all discipline seems painful rather than pleasant, but later it yields the peaceful fruit of righteousness to those who have been trained by it. Therefore lift your drooping hands and strengthen your weak knees, and make straight paths for your feet, so that what is lame may not be put out of joint but rather be healed.*

Our Heavenly Father asks us to remain childlike by trusting that His only desires are to grow us in our faith and bless us as His beloved children.

## CRAWL YOUR WAY UP

Galatians 5:7 - *"You were running well. Who hindered you from obeying the truth?"*

On a dreary Monday morning in February 2010, I sat down in front of my laptop with a mug of coffee nearby. The slate-grey sky matched my mood. Mondays are devotional writing days for me, and although I had a theme in mind, the words did not come easily. *Fight the good fight, do all you can do, be content to do what you can do, and leave the results in God's hands.* It would be a woefully short devotional if I didn't flesh out my thoughts. The thought of writing an encouraging devotional was daunting as I was dealing with some discouraging situations in my life that day.

After about an hour of writing and deleting the same sentence repeatedly, I abandoned all hope that I would write that morning. I reached for my television's remote control. I knew the 2010 Winter Olympics would be featured on my local station. At first, I was only mildly interested. Within moments, I was riveted to the screen. I am decidedly non-athletic, but God often speaks to me through the Olympics, and that morning was no exception.

I was drawn to a young Canadian snowboarder named Maelle Ricker. Maelle battled the snowy elements, the diabolically tricky course, her growing fatigue, and her inner doubts. Fog rolled in from the ocean, which caused many delays. During her first run, Maelle had a spectacular fall that completely took her off the course. She had a decision to make. She could give up her hopes for a medal, or she could go on. To go on, she would have to hop-skip her way up the next huge jump with her boots still attached to her snowboard.

Hand and foot, Maelle clawed her way back up the steep, man-made obstacle to relaunch her bid for a medal. Others had fallen before her, many fell after her, and all had chosen to disqualify. She took the hard road and made it up that hill, completing her run with a dismal time. As the day progressed, the fog thickened. There were several delays that threatened her chance of a second qualifying run. A sudden snow squall could completely ruin her day. She chose not to be discouraged even though she had no control of the weather.

The fog finally lifted, and the officials gave the go-ahead for the race to continue. Ice crystals fell on the course, making it very slick. Maelle sailed through the quarter and semi-finals, finding herself in the gold-medal race. The icy, steep, and curvy course defeated two racers in the final race and caused her third competitor to become excessively cautious. Maelle victoriously sped past the finish line to claim the gold medal, much to the delight of the thousands of Canadians packed in the stands below.

That morning, I was confronted with a mountain of my own, and I had a choice. I could crawl my way up that hill with the help and empowering grace of the Lord, or I could give up and take the easier path. The tempter whispered, "Someone else will take up the prayer burdens; someone else will take over your responsibilities; it doesn't matter. You really don't make that much of a difference, and there are others who sailed right over this mighty hill before you. Let them run the race; you know the price you'll pay. It's just not worth it."

I sensed God waited for my response to the temptation. I knew His preference. He hoped that I would fight my way out of the fog. The decision was mine. Taking a deep breath, I placed my trust in His word, and I willed myself to keep my eye on the prize. I chose not to allow my fears and self-doubts to veer me off course. I prayed for the grace needed to claw myself up my own mountain. By relying on His grace, He gives me the momentum to soar up and over each mountain that I face. My confidence rests in His power to see me through until I cross the finish line.

## *Now What Do We Do?*

When we walk into a place of victory after a prolonged walk of faith, we will face giants in our new territory. This is to be expected! The children of Israel not only faced the task of removing the inhabitants within the Promised Land, but they also faced a major shift in the way they lived their daily lives.

An entire generation grew accustomed to the supernatural provision of God as they wandered through the desert (Exodus 16:35, Deuteronomy 29:5). Six days a week, they easily gathered manna as it fell right outside their tents. On the seventh day, they ate from the abundance of the sixth. Their clothes didn't wear out; their shoes never needed repair.

Once they entered the Promised Land, God's supernatural provision stopped. They had to learn to hunt and gather food for themselves (Joshua 5:11). Skills long forgotten, such as weaving, sewing and leatherwork, now had to be used. They were called to be self-sufficient, and in the same breath, they were warned to remain humble and dependent on God's direction. If they did not heed God's commands, they would not take full possession of the land God gave them. If they did not learn to grow their food, they would die. They needed to co-labour with their Creator; they needed to learn to take personal responsibility for their lives.

If you feel inadequate for a task that lies before you, don't lose heart. Keep your eyes on Him, and He will guide you as you learn the skills needed to conquer the giants in the land.

## THE BIG STICK

I have quite a collection of big sticks. These destructive weapons are invisible, making them even more dangerous. You won't come across these weapons in a gun catalogue or a martial-arts studio, yet they carry a lethal blow if repeatedly used. These weapons cause great damage to the victim's spirit, soul and body. What makes them even more heinous is the fact that these weapons are used to inflict grievous self-harm. I have witnessed the devastating aftermath caused by these self-inflicted assaults in the lives of my friends and family. I have dealt with the aftermath of wielding a big stick against myself by retreating into the shadows, hoping no one sees my battle scars.

What is the name of this loathsome weapon?

Self-condemnation.

My definition of self-condemnation is the harsh judgment that we place upon ourselves, blanketing our whole being with lies that we are the worst person on the planet. We proclaim that we are so hopelessly flawed that it is impossible for us to find redemption. Condemnation attacks our character with broad and vague statements that offer no hope for our miserable condition.

We use our sticks of self-condemnation when we fall into repeated sin. When we experience failure and disappointment in our lives, we wield the big stick against ourselves. This barbaric approach does nothing to bring resolution and only results in scars that hinder us from receiving God's truth. Self-condemnation is the equivalent of dropping a nuclear bomb on a house in an attempt to get rid of a lone mouse in the attic. Overkill at its worst.

In contrast, God's weapon for dealing with sin is precise and effective. The sharp arrow of God's conviction targets the exact centre of a specific infection or fatal disease in our hearts. His conviction is never vague. When left in the hands of our skillful Surgeon, conviction always provides an avenue for healing, restoration, and freedom. As we repent of specific sins and determine not to return to our destructive behaviour, we will find true and lasting healing.

Hebrews 4:12 (MSG) - *"His powerful Word is sharp as a surgeon's scalpel, cutting through everything, whether doubt or defense, laying us open to listen and obey."*

I counsel my friends to step away from the big stick when they are tempted to grovel in self-condemnation. Might I offer you the same advice? Step away from the big stick! Allow the Holy Spirit to have exclusive access to those areas of your heart that might need a Surgeon's scalpel. You will find His hand is steadier than your own, and His surgery will bring lasting health and vigour to your soul.

## The First Signs of Spring

The annual first signs of spring begin to crop up in my city every March. The cycle of freezing and thawing of asphalt and roadways naturally results in potholes. When the road freezes, it expands, which causes cracks. When combined with the heavy wear and tear of a multitude of vehicles and the sudden and rapid temperature fluctuations, a pothole can form very rapidly. As snow and ice melts, the growth of the pothole accelerates. In a large urban centre in a northern climate, drivers and pedestrians must dodge and avoid these early reminders that the long winter will soon be over.

While this may sound easy in theory, it is not quite as simple in practice. Case in point: On a mild evening in early March a few years back, I felt restless and decided to head over to my local supermarket to pick up a few items. I traveled in autopilot along my tried and true favourite route as I mentally wrote a grocery list. I barely noticed a puddle in the left-hand turning lane of the street that I was about to cross, but it didn't look too deep. I didn't pay too much attention to it. I forged ahead and found myself stuck in the ice that lay just below the watery surface. Try as I might, I couldn't free myself by backing up or revving my power chair forward. Only with the help of a Good Samaritan was I able to free my chair and continue along my way.

I fell victim to my presumption that what was once a trouble-free path would always remain a trouble-free path. I had allowed myself to grow lax in my familiar settings, and I failed to stay alert to potential problems that might lie ahead.

I am a creature of habit, and I find comfort in familiarities and routines. I place my reading glasses in the same spot each night, and I always sleep on the same side of the bed. Bed manufacturers have found it much simpler to instruct their patrons to flip their mattresses every couple of months rather than try to persuade their patrons to change their sleeping patterns every now and again. Mattresses are more open to change, so it seems.

God, who created me, also created the seasons, the daily rising and setting of the sun, the predictable coming in and going out of the tide. He set forth His divine plan, bringing chaos into order. However, the same Lord cautions me not to place my confidence in the familiar as the familiar can lull me into a dangerous complacency. He wants me to stay alert and remain flexible, keeping my heart open to the changes He might add to my daily itinerary.

Proverbs 16:9 - *"The heart of man plans his way, but the Lord establishes his steps."*

## Mutual Appreciation Society

One Saturday, a friend and I travelled a short distance from my city to visit my much-loved elderly aunt. A few days earlier, a note arrived in my mailbox saying that my aunt missed me and wanted to see me, and I did everything in my power to find my way to her little retirement apartment.

Why did I make the effort to go? Because I knew I would be in the presence of someone who loved me unconditionally. I knew she would greet me with arms opened wide to give me a hug. I know I would be the recipient of her affectionate kisses, and I knew that I would come away feeling refreshed and loved. This visit was no exception. Although I brought an enormous bouquet of spring flowers, her eyes were only on me and not on my gift. I gently prodded her to unwrap the flowers, as she was too busy asking questions about my life and filling me in on the comings and goings of her children and grandchildren.

I felt right at home with my aunt, and she felt right at home with me. I found it easy to express my affection for her. It always was a mutual admiration society between my aunt and me. This particular visit was bittersweet. I noticed an oxygen tank in the corner by her electric wheelchair. I couldn't help but notice the frailty of her frame and the hollowness of her cheeks. I cherished every moment of that afternoon. I knew the days I could visit her this side of heaven were numbered.

My mind wandered back to the practical ways she loved me. She made the dress I wore on my very first day of school. Family pictures show me looking as proud as a princess in the tasteful little frock she designed just for me. I loved that dress! I remembered the Thanksgiving meals she served our extended family. My uncle and she would open up their steakhouse to us, spending their rare day off cooking up a magnificent feast. They served us all on fine china and crystal. As an impressionable child, I felt honoured to be served by such a glamorous couple! Although I was on my best behaviour, I confess that I broke a glass or two.

My aunt and uncle moved to the United States for a while, and my travels took me around the world. We didn't see each other very often. By coincidence, I eventually moved to the same city where they had relocated after my uncle's retirement. When they discovered I was living nearby, they immediately invited me over for a home-cooked meal. Every year, my aunt baked a magnificent carrot cake for my birthday that would have fed an army of twenty.

As we visited over a cup of coffee in her tiny retirement apartment, my aunt insisted I take her current copy of her favourite magazine. She just knew I'd love a particular story in that month's issue. When I vehemently protested, she insisted that I take it. Stubbornness runs deep in my family, and I wisely conceded, knowing that I would not win the battle that day. After all, how could I deny her anything? How could I not love this woman who loved me so much?

Although the love my aunt bestowed on me could never match the love the Lord lavishes on me, there are similarities. He, too, calls me to fellowship with Him. He loves to bestow me with His gifts. He invites me to share my heart with Him. He loves to hear all about my dreams and sorrows. He sees past my awkwardness, and He finds my imperfect demonstrations of affection endearing. How can I express to Him how grateful I am for every good gift He has given me? How can I possibly show my appreciation for His unmerited love for me? I suppose the only way I can is by answering His call when He beckons me to enter His presence.

## In It For The Long Haul

The proof that you love someone is not that you have warm, affectionate feelings toward him or her. The proof is in your actions, your words, and your sacrifice. Your willingness to give the best of yourself and your willingness to get nothing in return is the surest sign of agape love.

The Lord asks me to demonstrate this truth during seasons where otherwise healthy relationships are strained. As my friends and loved ones struggle with anxiety, stress, confusion, and pain, they are not able to see past their personal hurts. When they are incapable of giving me anything in return, God asks me to offer the hours that I spend in prayerful support to Him as a sacrifice.

When I am tempted to step away from painful relationships, I feel the Lord's persistent conviction to press on. Once, I asked the Lord for endurance to remain faithful to a friend who battled through a particularly difficult emotional crisis in her life. I grew weary; I had nothing more to give her beyond a listening ear. I was suffering from compassion fatigue. The extended phone calls, daily emails and long chats over a cup of coffee had taken their toll.

As I cried out for God's mercy on behalf of myself and my friend, I felt the Lord ask, "If your friend was struggling with a life-threatening physical illness, would you walk away?"

I believe the Lord does not want me to drown in the whirlpool of my friends' strife, and He has reminded me more than once that He is their Saviour and I am not. Nevertheless, He asks me to love my friends and family with the same sacrificial love He has extended toward me.

## ON THEM HAS LIGHT SHONE

Isaiah 9:2 - *"The people who walked in darkness have seen a great light; those who dwelt in a land of deep darkness, on them has light shone."*

In the late eighties, I worked with newcomers to Canada by helping them to acclimate to Canadian culture. As they often had to wait several months before attending English as a Second Language classes, I acted as a tutor. I taught them survival English and helped them learn practical skills, such as reading a bus map and how to shop the Canadian way.

One wintry December day, I was running late as the city buses were behind schedule due to heavy snowfall. As I trudged along a snow-covered sidewalk in the dusky twilight of an Edmonton winter afternoon, I hoped that I was not too late. I tried to visit newcomers in midmorning or mid-afternoon in the hopes that they would not feel culturally obliged to cook me a meal. Most of these families barely had enough for their family to eat, and they all relied on our local food bank. I knew that as it was 4:00 p.m., I was running the risk of being asked to stay for a meal, but the family I was visiting needed help deciphering their telephone bill.

This family of three sisters had a special place in my heart as they were all around my age. Two of the sisters were about as near-sighted as I was at the time, and we teased each other by comparing the thickness of our glasses' lens. Yes, on this cold, snowy day, I was looking forward to a hot cup of green tea and a good chat with my friends. After stomping my boots against the snow carpet in the vestibule of their apartment building, I buzzed their suite. There was no answer. I waited a minute or two, then buzzed again. Still no answer. I knew they were loath to leave their warm apartment. I buzzed once more, then sighed. It appeared I would not have that hot cup of tea after all.

As I wrapped my scarf around my face and headed down the sidewalk, I heard my name being shouted. One of the sisters frantically waved for me to come back. I stomped the snow off my boots, cleared the fog from my glasses, and then navigated my way down the stairs to their apartment. Now that I was able to see, I was startled to realize that my friend was in her pajamas!

Outside of the small glow of light provided by a study lamp on the kitchen table, their apartment was in darkness. "Are you sick?" I asked. "What about your sisters?" I peered in the living room, but I didn't see the girls there.

"Oh no!" She was swift to reassure me. "We were sleeping."

Sleeping at 4:15 p.m.? I wondered if they had started a new job, working nights.

"Oh no." She gestured out her window. "It is dark out, and so we went to bed. I forgot you were coming today!"

Sheepishly, her sisters joined us around the table and explained they had no other lamp in the house, except for the bathroom light. When my ministry organization moved them into their apartment, we hadn't checked to make sure the light worked in their bedroom. Apparently, there wasn't even a bulb in the light socket!

Taking advantage of a teachable moment, I wrote down the phrase they would need to use to buy bulbs. I did get my cup of tea after all. As we talked, I sensed a deep despair in all three sisters. After sending a silent prayer to God for wisdom, I used an English – Vietnamese dictionary and hand gestures until I eventually discerned the cause of their gloom. I began to ask some leading questions in the hopes of drawing them out of their shells.

One sister burst into tears as she gestured toward the night sky. All three sisters were crying now. What sort of country had they moved to? Would it always be so dark and snowy and cold? Had they made a mistake in coming? They had only been in Canada one month, and they just didn't think they could dwell in the land of eternal gloom. I passed around tissues, then refilled our tea cups as I waited for them to compose themselves.

I spoke from my many years of experience as a resident of Canada and reassured the girls that when June came around, they would be basking in comforting sunlight until 10:00 p.m. The sun would rise long before they awoke each morning. Although they would have to endure winter, summer would indeed come. After another cup of tea, they brightened up, and we ended my visit in laughter. I left them enough money for light bulbs, but I made a mental note to call a co-worker as soon as I returned home. We needed to find the girls some lamps!

My friends chose to believe my testimony, and they used that testimony to nurture and sustain hope in their hearts. They would not always have to bundle up in sweaters, parkas, scarfs, boots, and mittens to go grocery shopping. There would not always be snow and ice on the sidewalks. The sun would return! As their basement apartment faced the southeast, their home would be flooded with natural light. They would not always live in gloom.

God asks us to carry embers of His goodness and empowering light into dark places. As we share how God brought us out of the darkness and into the light, our words become vessels that carry hope to the listener. He will bring them through their dark season. He did it for us; He will do it for them. When we are in a dark season of our own, it is easy to refuse to believe that His light is on the horizon. It would be more beneficial to receive the embers of hope others carry to us by their testimony. Allow God to fan those precious embers of hope into flame.

## HE'S NOT DEAD YET!

*"I will not judge a person to be spiritually dead whom I have judged formerly to have had spiritual life, though I see him at present in a swoon as to all evidences of the spiritual life. And the reason I will not judge him so is this — because if you judge a person dead, you neglect him, you leave him; but if you judge him in a swoon, though never so dangerous, you use all means for the retrieving of his life."* John Owen

My heart rebels against judgmental statements that believers are apt to make against those who have reportedly fallen from grace. I regularly dismiss rumours of impropriety. On the occasion that my presumption of the accused's innocence is disproven, I do my best to deal with disappointment and to pray for the fallen and those who are wounded by their fall. I pray for grace and for a heart that desires reconciliation and restoration. Sometimes, it takes me longer to extend the same grace that I hope would be offered to me if I fell in similar circumstances.

I refuse to abandon hope that the prodigals in my life will return. As I live near the centre of my large urban city, I occasionally stumble across brothers and sisters in Christ with whom I once shared close fellowship. These lost individuals have wandered away from God, yet their Father has not abandoned them. I believe that God deliberately brings them along my path so I may convey His love, grace and hope to them.

I have choices to make when I run into these family members. I can remember the hurts they inflicted upon me. I can remember the wounds others inflicted on them. I can use these remembrances as an excuse to pretend I don't see them across a crowded supermarket or outdoor venue. I can choose to not approach them out of fear of being rejected.

On the other hand, I can approach them with a heart of sisterly love and affection without judgment or religious manipulation. A simple word of greeting, an offer of a cup of coffee on me, a smile and a hug will all go a long way toward reconciliation. A listening ear can open a wandering heart to the thought that God still loves them, and there just might be a place still set for them at their Father's table.

## *Inattentive Receiving*

Being disabled, I am often dependent on others. A constant frustration revolves around transportation. As my disability does not allow me to drive, I must rely on friends when my power chair can't go where I need to go. After several disastrous trips using my city's transportation system for the disabled, I realized that the service is wonderful for those who have routine daily trips. However, the system is not set up to fit in sporadic users such as myself.

As a result, I find myself going out less in the winter as I do not want to overburden those who graciously provide me rides. These faithful few go miles out of their way to give me a lift, and I hate taking advantage of their generosity. These same individuals stay late after Sunday morning church services to help tidy up. They arrive early to church to shovel the walks, and they are usually the ones who fill in the slack when others do not follow through on their commitments. I make it a practice to pray for these friends, asking the Lord to protect them from burnout. I pray for grace for their families and loved ones as they end up sacrificing precious family time on Sundays as a result. As they are already overtaxed, I try to find alternative rides.

On occasion, I struggle with resentment towards those who assume others will do what needs to be done. However, when I choose to resent those who do nothing, I fail to give thanks for those who do so much. When my attention remains on those who feel entitled to only consume, I fail to treasure His faithful ones.

When I am not able to attend church for a few weeks due to a lack of transportation, I remember the countless thousands of Christians around the world who do not have access to a local church. Furthermore, they do not have unlimited access to the Internet and all the resources I have available at my fingertips.

When I begin to fret that I have been stuck indoors for a couple of weeks without seeing a friendly face, I remember the disabled individuals I visited in my youth as a volunteer. Although they were young, they had no choice but to live in a nursing home due to their disability. They lived among the elderly and felt isolated and misunderstood. I count myself fortunate that I have close friends who stay in touch by text or email.

I have a Friend who is closer than a brother and who is my

constant Companion. The Lord's prescription for my ungrateful heart is not complicated. He asks me to choose to live each day from a place of intentional gratefulness. When my heart meditates on all that He has provided me through His death and resurrection, there is no room for churlishness. When I choose to make joy the foundation of my life, resentment and judgmental attitudes find no place in the dwelling of my heart.

## *A Winter's Caress*

On a cool November evening, I joined a group of mission students gathered for an impromptu bonfire in a protected gully at a Bible camp. The stars shone bright overhead and a full moon illuminated our path, so the flashlights we carried were not needed. As most of us were from the northern hemisphere, we were well acquainted with numb fingertips and reddened noses. Those who had gone ahead had the fire blazing by the time the rest of the troop arrived, and we gathered around the circle, sipping on hot chocolate as we shared our hearts with one another.

I was so caught up in the warm fellowship, the flickering flames, and crackling embers, a drizzle of a water drop startled me as it dripped from my hair onto my cheek. Gazing up, I saw huge, perfect fluffy snowflakes drift down from the sky, too numerous to even count. Lost in the beauty, I stepped back from the flames and continued to gaze upward.

The longer I gazed upward, the deeper my wonder became. An optical illusion caused by the shadow of the flakes falling into the light of the bonfire made it seem as if I were flying upward into the sky, shooting high among the stars. It seemed an eternity; it seemed a second; it was a timeless moment. My God and I. He blanketed the earth with His snowy glory, yet each snowflake that caressed my upturned face was a personal touch.

He covered the whole world with His love, yet He curled up within my heart with the soft, cool kiss of a snowflake.

## Shirley, Goodness and Mercy

I spent much of my tenth year of life in a children's hospital as I had casts on both legs, and I was wheelchair-bound. My father worked second or third shift, and my mother took care of four children at home, so they couldn't make it to the hospital every day to visit, and I was lonely. I missed my friends; I was lonely for my school. I missed my mother's dog even though he didn't like kids. Yes, I was homesick.

One Wednesday night, I was sitting alone on my bed. Most of the other children who shared my wardroom had visitors, and I had no one to talk to. Our community television was turned off during visiting hours. For once in my life, I found reading to be dull and lifeless. Try as I might, I couldn't lose myself in my latest Nancy Drew book, and even Anne of Green Gables failed to capture my imagination. There was an ache in me that needed filling.

Just as I was about to dissolve into tears, two cheerful women popped in the door. They were strangers to me but not to the nursing staff. The nurses announced that there was "Sunday School" in the sunroom for anyone who wanted to come. The beaming women gestured that all were welcome. I knew it was a Wednesday and not a Sunday. The thought that these two sweet ladies didn't seem to be aware of that fact intrigued me enough to muster the courage to ask to join. I soon found myself wheeled into the sunroom. Within minutes, our teachers had their little flock playing "Bible Twenty Questions" and gave us crayons and colouring sheets when the game was over. Although I felt that I was a bit too old to be colouring pictures, something in their hearts attracted me to their gentle message. At the end of the night, they taught us the simple chorus.

> "Surely Goodness and Mercy
> Shall follow me
> All the days,
> All the Days of my life
> And I will dwell in the House of the Lord
> Forever"

I had no idea who this "Shirley" was, and I had no idea why I was letting her know that goodness and mercy were following me around. However, somehow, I knew that Jesus was good, and He was merciful, and He loved children. I could hardly wait to learn more, but it was another two weeks before I was able to attend again. The women sensed that I was hungry for more of God and continued to teach about the love of Jesus. I believe that at that point, in childlike faith, I asked Jesus to be with me and be my Shepherd.

The next day when my mother came to visit, I excitedly told her everything that had transpired the preceding evening. She forbade me to go to another Sunday School class and informed the nurses that because another denomination oversaw the meeting, I was not allowed to attend. She didn't her daughter to have anything to do with religion that was not her own. Since that time, my mother has changed her views!

Although I never saw those two women again, God took me at my word, and He became my good Shepherd. I had no idea I was supposed to read my Bible, and even if I had known I needed to read it, I wouldn't have known where to find one. He kept me safe. The Holy Spirit convicted me of sin. His voice warned me of danger. I have no doubt that it was only by His sustaining grace that I made it through many traumatic years in a dysfunctional family setting.

I remember that on several occasions, I felt an overwhelming urge to flee from a situation, only to find out later that trouble started a few moments after I left. I didn't have a conscious prayer life outside of the rigid formality of my denomination. Although for a time I forgot I was one of His sheep, He never forgot that He was my Shepherd.

At the age of seventeen, I deepened my relationship with God during a high school youth retreat. A few months after my encounter with Christ, I was cast in a play where the entire cast sang the chorus that I learned so many years earlier. I couldn't remember where I had learned it as many of my memories were locked away at that point in my life due to my traumatic upbringing. All I knew is that the song brought me comfort.

It wasn't until I was well into my thirties that I remembered the two friendly women and their message of love. Suddenly, it all made sense. I now knew why I managed to survive my challenging teen years. My Shepherd led me, and His mercy and goodness followed behind me.

Never discount even the briefest of encounters you might have with those around you. A simple song, a loving hug, a listening ear, or a simple prayer can capture a wounded heart and woo it to Jesus. I am sure those Sunday School teachers had no idea of the ripple effect they had on my life, but I am very grateful for their obedience and their willing hearts.

## Laying Down Our Crowns

I struggle with the idea of receiving a crown in heaven. I picture myself handling the thing like a hot potato, tossing it as soon as possible before the throne. I don't like being in the spotlight and have always squirmed at the thought of standing before a crowd to receive accolades. I can barely sit through people singing "Happy Birthday" to me, and my friends love to tease me by prolonging my agony every year by serenading me with increasingly raucous renditions of the song.

One Sunday morning, God brought up the subject of crowns to me through the lyrics of a worship song. I inwardly rebelled, "God, I don't even look good in hats, I would look ridiculous wearing a crown!" I felt the Spirit's gentle nudge of conviction, wrapped in wry humour. "Well, for all the fuss you make about not wanting a crown, you sure like wearing them!"

Immediately, I thought of all the areas of my life in which I struggle to give over full control to God. I thought of family members and friends, my finances, my calendar, my privacy, my comfortable routines. Although I know God is faithful and is much more able to rule over those areas in my life, I am often reluctant to remove myself from the throne and allow Him to sit in His proper place.

Perhaps like me, you are a pretender to the throne, and God is politely asking you to step aside so He, the rightful Ruler, can take His place. Maybe He is giving us the opportunity to practice the laying down of our crowns now so we won't look foolish in heaven. After all, anyone who has been asked to throw the first ceremonial pitch at a baseball game knows, "Practice makes perfect."

## *I Was Homesick*

Monsoon rains, flooded roads, and dreary, oppressive clouds contributed to my despondency one year when I was thousands of miles from home. It was Christmas 1983, and I was in rural Hawaii. Christmas in Hawaii may seem like a tropical paradise to some but not to a Canadian girl who had not seen her family for a couple of years.

I missed the sound of snow crunching under my boots. I missed the insulating blanket of snow that contributed to the reverent silence that always enveloped me as I left Christmas Eve services in snowy Alberta. I wistfully looked out the foggy window of my Hawaiian dorm room. In my mind's eye, I could see my family's crowded dining-room table as the steam from a turkey dinner clouded the windows and obscured the view of a sunny, crisp December winter day. I could almost hear the tried and true family jokes and the quick cracking pop as Christmas crackers were snapped open. I chuckled at the memory of my conservative grandparents wearing silly paper hats that tumbled out of the crackers. I even missed the green Jell-O and mayonnaise salad my mother made every year. No one had the courage to tell her that we really didn't like it much. It was tradition. It was home.

With a sigh, I turned away from the window. I was celebrating the holiday in a foreign land. Our Christmas tree was a single palm frond, decorated with a couple of popcorn strands. Despite their personal bouts of homesickness, the people around me were gracious and kind, but they just weren't family. As I left our impromptu worship service, I trudged through ankle-deep mud caused by constant monsoon rains. Instead of a parka, I wore a rain poncho. We had a lovely meal together, but it just wasn't the same. There was no green Jello-O salad. Nothing felt right, and everything seemed out of alignment. I was a stranger.

Decades later, while I was in worship one Sunday, I felt the same homesickness wash over me. I realized that I was homesick for my heavenly home. I longed for a face-to-face chat with Father God. I wanted to sit beside my older brother, Jesus, and hear Him laugh as He told the stories of His day. I wanted it to be easy; I wanted to be understood by people who spoke my heart language.

I long for the day when I can sit at the wedding feast of the Lamb and join in the celebration. I long to share the inside jokes that only a family can appreciate. Perhaps John will regale us with humorous tales of fishing trips with Peter and Andrew. Perhaps we'll gently rib Zacchaeus about his tree-climbing antics.

God has not yet released me to come home. I am still in His service and a member of His diplomatic corps. My mission is not yet completed. There are times I feel I am a stranger in a strange land, but God has placed me here to be His ambassador, representing His kingdom and inviting those around me to join His family. He has not left me without comfort! I have the immediate and intimate contact with my Father God and my brother Jesus. Whenever I need His advice, I can open one of my 'letters from home' and find words of wisdom to guide me through whatever I am facing. I will remain faithful in His service, looking forward to that day when I am welcomed home for eternity.

*"Home is the one place in all this world where hearts are sure of each other. It is the place of confidence. It is the place where we tear off that mask of guarded and suspicious coldness which the world forces us to wear in self-defense, and where we pour out the unreserved communications of full and confiding hearts. It is the spot where expressions of tenderness gush out without any sensation of awkwardness and without any dread of ridicule."* - Frederick W. Robertson

## GIVE FROM WHAT YOU'VE BEEN GIVEN

Mark 12: 42-44 – *"And He sat down opposite the treasury and watched the people putting money into the offering box. Many rich people put in large sums. And a poor widow came and put in two small copper coins, which make a penny. And He called His disciples to him and said to them, "Truly, I say to you, this poor widow has put in more than all those who are contributing to the offering box. For they all contributed out of their abundance, but she out of her poverty has put in everything she had, all she had to live on.*

As a child, I gave my mother a beautiful bouquet of bright, yellow flowers every year. She would then put them in a little glass by the kitchen sink. "So I can look at them when I'm washing dishes," she'd say. I would watch her arrange them in an old tumbler glass that was set aside for such bouquets. I was happy to see the smile on my mother's face.

Across North America, countless mothers receive similar bouquets of weeds from their preschoolers. Although the sight of a yard full of dandelions is dismaying to most adults, the same crop is a never-ending supply of riches to a child. The bright, sunny petals are a delight to their young eyes. If the truth would be told, most mothers find as much joy in a drooping bouquet made of dandelions delivered by a toddler as a dozen roses delivered by the local flower shop.

And so it is with God. Are you reluctant to present a gift to Him because you consider it unworthy? Have you held back from placing your offering at His feet because you compare your gift to the gifts that others have already laid there? Have you stopped short of responding to pastoral a call for help, even as your heart pounded, and you were sure your pastor was looking right at you when He asked for volunteers for a church project? Have you kept your tongue when the Holy Spirit prompted you to share with another believer, out of fear of saying something wrong?

Step out and watch how the Lord works through the weak and the lowly. He loves to take the gifts we give Him, empowering us with His strength and transforming our gift with His light. The Lord only asks us to give Him our hearts and for us to walk in obedience and trust. He will never reject a gift given to Him from a heart of love.

## *Watching Them Soar*

A lonely, young mother, who I will call Sheryl, stumbled across an Internet chat room I managed in the 1990s. Sheryl fled her homeland as a refugee along with her husband and two children. Homesick and heartsick, she worried for those she left behind in her native country as they faced starvation and oppression. Shortly after her arrival, Sheryl learned that her father back home was gravely ill, and doctors could do nothing to help him. Many medical professionals had already fled the country, leaving the healthcare system in shambles. Her parents were divorced, and her mother was in a dangerous living situation. Members of Sheryl's home church were starving. Store shelves were empty. Sending money would not help her loved ones as there was nothing left to buy. Sheryl's dormant eating disorder awakened. Now her health was at stake.

Sheryl was a stranger in a new country and had not yet found a home church. She felt isolated, having little fellowship outside of the Internet friends she had met in our chat room. As her spiritual battle raged on, we prayed. When she despaired, we spoke hope into her life. We encouraged her to seek the help she needed, but shame kept her bound. We doubled our efforts in prayer. Ever so slowly, cracks began to appear in her walls of guilt and shame, and they began to crumble. One day, Sheryl broke down and reached out to her husband. Together, they sought help from the local medical community.

God was waiting for her and placed Christian doctors and therapists at the inpatient eating disorder centre nearby. Her main counsellor happened to be from the same country she had just fled and understood her pain. God was on the move! Through prayer, determination, and hard work, freedom's bell started to ring for Sheryl. She completed treatment and gained employment with a Christian firm. Her family found friendship in a local church where she was baptised beside her husband. Their family was embraced by a loving circle of friends.

As her health improved, Sheryl had an abundance of physical energy and emotional strength. She rejoiced that she was able to watch her children play sports and quickly became a minivan-driving soccer mom just like any mother in the nation she now called home. As she stepped out into her new life, she stepped away from our little cyber-community. Although I missed her, I rejoiced in her freedom.

That's the bittersweet joy of ministry. We see people healed, and then we watch them move on to victory. Sometimes, it means saying goodbye. We must learn to celebrate as our fledgling birds spread their wings and fly into freedom, even if that flight pattern takes them far away from us.

## THERE IS ALWAYS THE PROMISE OF DAYLIGHT

Hosea 6:3 - *"Let us know; let us press on to know the Lord; his going out is sure as the dawn; he will come to us as the showers, as the spring rains that water the earth."*

Living in north-central Alberta, I find February to be difficult. Although the calendar promises that spring is a mere six or seven weeks away, the truth is, spring won't take place for at least another two months. I am held captive by the dead of winter. The comfort of Christmas is far behind me. The days are short; the weather is bone-chilling cold. Icy sidewalks and roads have no opportunity to melt naturally. There are always a few people who refuse to clear their sidewalks. As a result, I am often trapped on my block, unable to grocery shop because my power chair can't navigate through deep snow or ice-blocked sidewalk corners.

As a result, I am isolated for weeks at a time. Although I am naturally an introvert, albeit a talkative one, I struggle with melancholy and self-pity on the gloomiest of days. I thank God for the weapons He provides for me to use against these destructive and dangerous foes. The joy of the Lord is one weapon. As I deliberately choose to rejoice, He strengthens me. Even when I find it difficult to be thankful within my own circumstances, God is faithful to remind me where my strength lies.

During the long winter, I am often given the opportunity to rejoice with a friend when they can escape the harsh weather for a week or two. I have a choice; I can rejoice with them, or I can grumble to myself, only deepening the chill and darkness of my winter experience. I have the choice; I can be jealous of their blessing, or I can choose to align my heart with their testimony of hope.

In contrast to Canada's winter, February is midsummer in Australia and New Zealand. Many of my Aussie and Kiwi friends use Facebook to share photographs and stories of their camping trips and outings to the beach. While I allow myself a certain measure of wistful 'I wish I were there' moments, I genuinely give thanks for God's blessings in their lives. As I pour over their photos and read their stories, I bask in the sun along with them. My faith is strengthened, because I know that the same God who blesses them will bless me in due season.

When friends experience a great harvest in their lives, I rejoice in their blessing, no matter what my personal circumstances may be. I know that the spring rain that falls upon them will eventually fall on me, washing off the soot and grime. If I remain faithful and pure of heart, I will see the promise of new life and new growth in the small seedlings that lie dormant in my heart during my personal winter. I have learned that bitterness, resentment, and self-pity do nothing to lift the gloomy clouds of a spiritual February in my life. If anything, these sins only harden the soil of my heart, making it difficult for new growth to spring forth at God's appointed time.

## THE LIVING IS EASY

*"Summertime, and the livin' is easy, Fish are jumpin' and the cotton is high"* - DuBose Heyward

As a child, I endured the winter and lived in hope for the summer. Swimming lessons, late night games of tag, days spent under a shade tree as I devoured book after book. The heady scent of flowers, the soothing sound of busy insects in the distance and the tinkle of the ice cream peddler's bell as he cycled through the neighbourhood. Those hazy, lazy blur of days that melted into weeks that flowed into months.

Upon my return to school, I would be hard-pressed to answer that age-old essay question, "What did you do this summer?" Not only did I have little to report, but I also found it hard to keep focused on the task assigned. In my pursuit of doing nothing over the summer, I had neglected the practice of being diligent.

Once I began to volunteer for various agencies during my summers, I found I finally had something to write about in my yearly essay. I found my summers to be more fulfilling. My time off was treasured, I felt I had accomplished something, and I found the return to the discipline of schoolwork was not overwhelming.

When we are in a season where all is right in our world, and there is no apparent battle looming, it is easy to sit back and allow our days to unfold before us. During such times of ease, we are the most vulnerable to the enemy's temptation and distraction. We are prone to compromise and procrastinate. If we are not careful, we find ourselves drifting into spiritual slumber. This gladdens our enemy's heart. He knows when we are in such a state, our spiritual reflexes are slow, our discernment is cloudy, and the weapons of our warfare are rusty from disuse.

Let us remain attentive and awake. Let us not turn away from our daily disciplines during times of ease so we do not fall out of the practice of hearing His voice. Let us keep the weapons of our warfare sharp, rust-free and ready for battle.

## Taste and See That the Lord is Good

"Chew each bite 20 times before swallowing. Put your fork down on your plate between each bite. Don't shovel your food!" Generations of parents at dinner tables across the world have offered this sage advice. Medical studies support these admonitions. Those who eat quickly and do not chew their food well will run a higher risk of obesity. Eating too quickly means the body will consume more calories than it requires before the brain feels satisfied. Chewing food releases enzymes in the mouth that aid the digestive process, and help to suppress the appetite.

Frustrated cooks watch with dismay as meals that took hours to prepare are devoured in mere moments. They shake their heads as carefully seasoned casseroles and soups are slathered with ketchup, salt and pepper by family members who don't bother to taste their food first. Husbands meet colourful salads and artistically arranged vegetable dishes with disdain and children ask if there is any dessert. Teens would rather eat instant noodles while playing their video games. Adults mindlessly munch on junk food as they watch the news. Children are handed a juice box and a sweetened granola bar while being loaded into a minivan on their way to soccer practice. Mothers stop at the local coffee shop for coffee and doughnuts, and then berate themselves for such poor nutritional habits. It is easy to understand why many home chefs turn to fast food take-out menus.

Our fast-paced culture has become a snare to many modern Christians. As we zip through our work schedules, church responsibilities and home life, we are so busy anticipating the next activity that we fail to give our full attention to the present moment. By lunchtime, we are focused on tomorrow's calendar, and we are hard-pressed to remember what we ate for breakfast. We are so busy looking for the next exit along the super highway of life that we have no idea where we have just been.

The Lord reminded me to slow down as I read Psalm 34:8, *"Taste and see that the Lord is good."* He brought me back to a cherished moment that took place in 1985 when I joined a group of fellow missionaries on a pleasure trip to central Thailand. Familiar rice paddies gave way to rolling hills and lush forests. As we reached the top of a particularly steep incline, I was met with one of the most beautiful landscapes I had ever seen. I whipped out my camera and took a desperate snapshot, knowing I did not have the time to set up proper composition for the frame. In the split second it took our van to navigate around the bend, I willed myself to slow that moment in my mind and to capture every detail of the breathtaking vista. I saw that view for a scant second that afternoon, but years later; I remember every detail of that magical valley, the wandering vines and the flora-covered rock formations.

I didn't allow that moment to slip past me like a half-chewed bite of hamburger. I savoured every morsel of the gift God gave me that day, and I have used the same technique over the years. I don't need a photo at hand or a note to jostle my memory; treasured moments are engrained deep in my heart, embossed by grateful attentiveness.

God calls me to "taste and see that He is good." I can only taste of His goodness if I take the time to savour that goodness. I will only discover the flavours and nuances of His goodness by being willing to explore flavours that might be unfamiliar to my spiritual palate. I must make a concerted effort to stay in the present moment; whether that be in reading His Word, talking with a friend, listening to a sermon, or enjoying His creation. Physical food nourishes us best when slowly and mindfully eaten, and the same holds true for those truths He speaks to our hearts.

## HE IS THE AIR I BREATHE

Acts 17:24-28

There are seasons when God seems very distant. In the midst of such trials, it is tempting to doubt that God truly carries our best interests at heart. We might even question the foundations of our faith, wondering if we have only deceived ourselves with the notion of a loving God who intervenes on behalf of His children. In those dark times, the dark night of the soul, as John of the Cross put it, we might question the reality of daylight.

Contrary to our fleeting emotions and doubting hearts, God has not wandered away leaving us to our own devices. The truth remains – every breath we take is a gift given by Him. Even in our darkest moments, when our emotions are numb, our hands are feeble, and our eyes are dim, God has not ceased to be God. His promises have not failed, and He still surrounds us.

Although we are seldom aware of our dependence on the physical oxygen that fills our lungs several times a minute, that oxygen never dissipates and is always there, waiting for our next breath. Although we do not always feel the air that surrounds us, we are always enveloped by air. We are God's children, and our survival depends on Him alone. In Him we live and move and have our being (Acts 17:28). Although we may not feel God's presence at times, we are always enveloped in God.

## WHAT'S A LITTLE SNOW GOING TO HURT?

Living in a northern climate, I consider myself a hearty person and well able to withstand the elements. There is a certain camaraderie in my neighbourhood that stands out during the winter months. You might think minus 15 C weather would cause my city to drop to its knees. Not so. Seniors bundle up and sport ice picks on their canes and place snow grips on their sturdy winter boots. Teens saunter down the sidewalk trying to act tough but only succeed in looking miserable and cold by leaving their coats wide open. Even a few joggers can be seen making their way past disability scooters, walkers, and wheelchairs.

One winter, the steady stream of pedestrians along a major thoroughfare in my city hit a snag and slowed to a crawl. On one side of the avenue, a major construction site routinely blocked the sidewalk as monster trucks loaded and unloaded equipment. On the other side was a large stretch of unshovelled sidewalk. After several snowfalls, the sidewalk became impassable for anyone who was unsteady on their feet or who relied on a wheelchair or stroller. Able-bodied pedestrians bypassed the icy mess by using the snowy lawn as a detour.

Several residents complained to city hall as city bylaws stated that sidewalks must be cleared within forty-eight hours of a snowfall. Volunteer agencies were available to shovel the walks of the elderly and the infirm. There was no excuse for non-compliance. Eventually, the sidewalk was cleared, and it looked as if a city crew had done it.

If the property owner had shovelled their walks after each snowfall, the task would have been simple. However, their negligence resulted in the sidewalk becoming compacted with ice, slush, and snow that formed hard ridges and deep ruts. Perhaps the owner did not realise how impassable his sidewalk had become, as most people used the back entrance to come and go from his building. Perhaps snowdrifts blocked his view of the sidewalk. What you can't see can't hurt you, after all.

It is easy to try to convince yourself, "As long as I am not hurting anyone, why should procrastination be wrong? Things will take care of themselves." When we do not deal with sin in our lives, each new sin builds upon our previous sin, eventually creating a danger not only to ourselves but to anyone else who would cross our path.

Let's keep short accounts with God and man, keeping our pathways clear and without stumbling blocks!

## Let a Fresh Breeze In!

Humans are creatures of habit, and Christians are no exceptions to the rule. Attend any given church for more than a year, and you will discover this to be true. The regulars all have their favourite place to sit. In some congregations, to sit in the unofficially official pew of an old faithful member is tantamount to heresy. Even the most anti-liturgical fellowship has a recognizable rhythm. Everyone knows approximately what time worship ends and how long the sermon will be. The congregation finds their beloved pastor's voice to be reassuring as he delivers his message in somewhat the same fashion week after week, month after month.

Many pastors look upon their Bibles as dear, familiar friends they are loath to retire, often choosing to rebind them. When they finally do buy a new Bible, most complain that they can't find a thing until the book has properly been broken in.

There is nothing inherently wrong with finding comfort in the familiar. However, when we obstinately stay within our comfort zone, we place ourselves at risk of missing all that God would have for us. When we offhandedly dismiss the unfamiliar, we deny ourselves the opportunity to remain teachable and open to the new things God wants to teach us.

Most of my friends would consider me quite cautious. I would characterize myself as stubborn and resistant to change at one point in my life. If a preacher was excessively enthusiastic in his preaching style, I tended to withdraw and found it difficult to receive his message. If a church embraced a certain style of worship music that didn't quite fit my personal musical taste, I found it difficult to enter the throne room, and I detoured to the judge's panel instead. I recognize my weaknesses and have done my best to work on these areas. However, to say that I still prefer the familiar over the unfamiliar would be an understatement.

Youth With A Mission staff and students are encouraged to keep our minds open to new cultures and to keep our hearts open to other streams of Christian expression. Our leadership realized that most of us would not necessarily stumble in our acceptance of local cultural expressions in the streets and parks of the country where we would be ministering. No, they knew we would find most of our cross-cultural difficulties to arise from within our team and through our interactions with the local Christians.

One lecturer gave the following illustration, an illustration that I have used countless times since. He asked us to visualize an open kitchen window, with its screen shut firmly in place, allowing fresh air to circulate through the room while keeping out the flies and pests. The speaker explained, "God asks us to keep the windows of our heart and mind open to all expressions of Christian faith while using the screens of wisdom and godly discernment the Holy Spirit provides. Allow those screens to keep out anything that would not be of Him." He went on to urge us, "Look past the style and look for the heart's intent."

Perhaps you tend to keep the storm shutters of your heart firmly in place. Perhaps you find it difficult to entertain the thought that anything new could be of God. Allow the image of a gentle, fresh breeze blowing through a room long shut off from any air circulation to entice you toward opening the windows to your heart. Entrust the Holy Spirit to be your screen of discernment.

## *Head for the Lifeboat!*

If the world's ship is sunk, and we as believers are in the lifeboat, are we helping to rescue those who are drowning around us? Are we encouraging and aiding them to scramble up to safety? I wonder.

Many believers are attending a huge party, thanking their divine Captain for saving them, but they are making so much noise, they can't hear the cries of those begging for a hand up into the lifeboat! Others lean over the edge of the boat busily bashing anyone in reach with their blanket judgments, pet doctrines, end-time theologies, and carefully memorized scripts. When their rescue techniques prove unsuccessful, these would-be heroes shake their heads in sorrow, bemoaning the hardhearted, unreceptive hearts of those who drown around them.

It seems many Christians are quick to condemn the world and write off its inhabitants as lost causes. It's odd though, Jesus never did. He healed, lovingly confronted, and walked among the lost, showing them the way to safety. Consistently, He engaged those who opposed Him by choosing His words and actions carefully – always in consideration of the audience He hoped to reach. His intention was to breathe life into the hearts of those He touched.

John 12:44-50 - And Jesus cried out and said, "Whoever believes in me, believes not in me but in him who sent me. And whoever sees me sees him who sent me. I have come into the world as light, so that whoever believes in me may not remain in darkness. If anyone hears my words and does not keep them, I do not judge him; for I did not come to judge the world but to save the world. The one who rejects me and does not receive my words has a judge; the word that I have spoken will judge him on the last day. For I have not spoken on my own authority, but the Father who sent me has himself given me a commandment —what to say and what to speak. And I know that his commandment is eternal life. What I say, therefore, I say as the Father has told me."

## Go into Egypt

Although it's hard to pinpoint the actual timeframe, Biblical scholars agree that the wise men visited Jesus at least several weeks after His birth. Joseph and Mary were staying in Bethlehem and living under fear and oppression.

Joseph worried about how he would support his young wife and her son. He knew Mary needed the love and advice of her family. Far away from his usual source of income, he had little financial means to support his family. Joseph's longed to return home. Back in Nazareth, he could financially support his family, he would be back in familiar surroundings, and he would feel more in control of the destiny of his family.

God knew better. He knew that Nazareth was not yet the place of safety for His Son, and so He spoke to Joseph through a dream. Within that dream, an angel instructed Joseph to head in the opposite direction of the security of home. Not only was God telling him not to return to the familiarity of the past, but God was also telling him to abandon his temporary place of refuge. God was sending this little family into a nation that had kept His people captive for centuries.

Joseph had a choice. He could dismiss the dream as a nightmare born out of the stress of his living situation, or he could step in faith and walk in obedience to the word of the Lord. I can imagine Joseph laying quietly in bed, glancing over at his wife and his adopted newborn son. He wondered how on earth he would explain to Mary that they were leaving Bethlehem and heading toward a hostile, foreign land.

Joseph walked in obedience to God despite his natural fears. Joseph chose to trust in the God who chose him to father His beloved Son. He chose obedience above his natural desire as a husband to provide for his wife and child.

In the midst of great uncertainty, our natural tendency is to try to control our environment and command our destiny. As followers of Jesus, we are commanded to surrender our destiny into the hands of our Lord.

God's perspective is broader than our own, Time and turmoil don't limit Him. Circumstances don't cloud His vision. He sees the whole picture, and when we turn to Him in trust and obedience, He promises that He will lead us. His intention is only to bless.

As we place our anxiety and fear into the hands of the One who knows our future and who knows what lies beyond our vision, He will not fail us.

## HIS MIRROR NEVER LIES

It was one of those days that left me shaken. Throughout the day, the Lord challenged me to remain faithful to Him. He asked me to stay open and transparent while allowing Him to be my Defender when necessary. He asked me to resist the urge to defend myself as a trio of confrontational situations arose within hours of each other.

Although each situation was unique, a common thread carried through. In each case, God needed me to step aside so He could be my advocate and advisor. He further advised me to take ownership of my sin by taking full responsibility for it, and He strongly suggested that I ask forgiveness from those involved without excusing my behaviour.

How I rebelled against admitting I am wrong! How my pride stung! My childish, sinful self rose to the surface, and I was sorely tempted to point an accusatory finger at the other party. My advocate's antidote for my pride was to hold a mirror up to my heart. I could only look for a moment; it is always painful to see oneself in the mirror of God's conviction. That mirror doesn't allow us to see ourselves in any other way but how God sees us. However, that brief glimpse was more than enough. I was swift to humble myself and admit my guilt.

As I apologized that day, I was sure that the next time I was tempted in these areas, I would not stumble. Unfortunately, I have had a few relapses along the way, but God faithfully alerts me when my attitude and behaviour are leading me towards sin. There is no such thing as an inconsequential sin in God's eyes. He knows all sin brings heart infection, spiritual illness, and death.

On the third occasion, I was thrust into a disagreement between friends. Both sides demanded I move in and pick sides. Both sides felt they were in the right; I felt both sides were in the wrong. It took a bit of fancy footwork, but I was able to step out of the ring, refusing to referee a situation that needed no third-party involvement.

Emotionally spent at the end of the day, I curled up on the couch and enjoyed a quiet moment before bed. I praised God for His infinite patience with His quarrelsome, finger-pointing, immature children. I thanked Him for the cross; I thanked Him for His unconditional love despite my sin, and I thanked Him that He loved me too much to allow me to stay in that sinful state. I thanked Him for growing me up just a wee bit more and for continuing the process of transforming me into His image. How I long to be a mirror that reflects His glory!

## *Sow Gratitude*

Although I don't have a garden of my own, and I am certainly not a farmer, I believe I know enough about the idea of cultivating to be confident in saying, cultivation requires work. A smattering of an occasional handful of seeds tossed onto the surface of untilled soil will not result in much of a crop, no matter how well-intentioned a momentary impulse to sow good seed might be. I have several friends who have lush, beautiful gardens, which is not an easy feat in north-central Alberta. Throughout the year, I overhear their conversations as they speak of tilling, composting, seedlings and planting, weeding and harvesting. Every step along the way demands their complete attention and conscious involvement to ensure a bountiful harvest.

And so, it is in growing a thankful heart. Wise parents instil in their toddlers the importance of saying please and thank you. Thoughtful parents add to this foundation by encouraging their young ones to draw thank-you pictures and write thank-you letters. It is hoped that the seeds of gratitude that are planted in childhood will continue to mature, moving past merely giving thanks for gifts that are received.

A healthy, flourishing grateful heart will see a reason to give thanks in all things, and it will give thanks in every season, no matter how dark and dreary those seasons may appear. A grateful heart sees with eyes of faith that which is yet to spring forth even in the long, dormant days of a spiritual winter.

When you cultivate a garden of praise and thankfulness you feast from its harvest.

## Do We Know Him?

I hope you will forgive me for the following flight of fancy. Although we know Him as Lord and Saviour, we might not know Him with the ease of familiarity that is only possible through much time spent in the presence of a loved one.

"Hello?"

"Daughter?"

"Yes?"

"Hi there, it's Jesus. I hope I didn't catch you at a bad time."

"Oh, no! Of course not, Lord. I was just reading about You. It's something John wrote. I can read it anytime, I guess. I was getting to the good part, though. Anyhow, what can I do for You? Did I ever tell You that I am so thankful for all You did for me? I don't know how I'd ever repay You. I mean, have You ever read what John said about you? It absolutely rocks!"

"Well, I was hoping we could get together, just you and me.

That is, if you're not too busy."

"I'd love that, Lord! Let me look at my calendar. I've got my poetry club with David on Monday night. Tuesday night, Solomon is giving a seminar on wisdom; I was really looking forward to that. Wednesday, Isaiah, you know him? He's going to be taking us on a treasure hunt, giving us clues to the Messiah. Oh right, that's You, so You'd know all about that. Thursday, I'm doing this real interesting study on Revelation with John. Friday, let me check … maybe, well, to be honest, I've meant to read Paul's letter to the Ephesians, meaty stuff in there! All about being in Christ in heavenly places... Oh right, You're seated up there, aren't you?"

"Well, you're studying all about me is wonderful, and those are all great people you mentioned. I love them all; they are part of my family, but I'd really like you to get to know me a bit better and not just know about me. Daughter?"

"Yes, Lord?"

"How about it? Just you and I, let's get together. I've got some parables I'd love to give you insight into as you read them in My presence. I think you'll find what I've got to say to be pretty helpful with those new challenges in your life. I've got some pointers on how to handle your money and how to deal with those troublesome neighbours of yours, too. While we're at it, I'd love to pray for you. You know the night I was praying for John and the other disciples? I was praying for you that night as well. You are constantly in my thoughts."

"Thanks for praying for me, and it's been far too long, just you and Me. I'd love to spend some time sitting at your feet and listening to what you have to say. But, Lord?"

"Yes, daughter?"

"Forgive me. I've been so busy learning about You that I've neglected to hear directly from the horse's mouth if You'll pardon the expression."

"Daughter?"

"Yes, Lord?"

"Of course I forgive you, and I pardon you for the expression as well."

## What's Yours is Mine, What's Mine is Mine

"His piece is bigger than mine!" "I want that red crayon right now, and I don't want him to have a turn with it." "It's not fair, Johnny has a super-turbo blaster, and I don't have one, so he has to give it to me. It's mine!" "What's mine is mine, and what's yours is mine, so hand it over now!" While self-centred attitudes might be expected at such a young age, such attitudes are best stopped by loving and firm redirection.

If children are not taught the value of sharing the fruits of their good fortune with others along with the art of rejoicing with others at their achievements or blessings, they tend to become insecure. These children grow to be embittered, frustrated, and disillusioned adults. Temper tantrums of a toddler are meet with more tolerance than the tantrums of a grown adult. Especially an adult who rails at a world that refuses to bend to their misbelief that they are entitled to as much, if not more, than the rest of the world.

As we mature in our faith, God encourages us to set aside such childish, selfish behaviour. Jesus uses the parable of the workers in the vineyard in Matthew 20:1-16 to bring this truth home.

Those he hired early in the day saw the landowner's generous wage as a fair bargain. They were grateful for his generosity up to the moment they realized that those hired in the last hour of the workday received the same generous wage. Suddenly, the fair bargain was no longer just in their eyes. Their personal circumstances had not changed; their employer did not reduce their salaries to pay the newcomers, yet they allowed envy and jealousy to overshadow the joy they once felt.

Jesus addressed this attitude through the story of the elder son in Luke 15:11-32. The son always had access to his father's wealth, cattle, and favour, yet failed to take advantage of all that was at his disposal. It was only upon his younger brother's triumphant return to the family fold that the elder brother complained of his father's perceived favouritism.

Father God, we confess we have no need to feel insecure or jealous of our brothers and sisters in Christ. We ask Your forgiveness as we have not recognized the unmerited favour You have lavished upon us. We thank You for Your unending, abundant supply of grace and love. Give us hearts that join in the song of thanksgiving as others celebrate the blessings in their lives. We thank You for intentional gratitude, for it will protect our hearts from the poisons of envy and jealousy.

## CLEAR YOUR CLOSET

I had an idea for a devotional in mind, but I was fretting and fussing. I wasn't sure how to word what I wanted to say. Turning to the Internet for inspiration, I typed in a few keywords. Lo and behold, I found the perfect quote that echoed my thoughts. There was only one problem. It was a quote from a devotional I published several years before!

Although I chuckled at my absentmindedness, it got me thinking. In previous days, I found myself disturbed by a rash of reality television programs centering on the world of storage locker auctions and pickers. These people make their living by rummaging through people's junk that has been stored away for decades in outbuildings, basements and attics.

The majority of people rent storage lockers for legitimate reasons such as temporary homelessness and floods. They might rent a locker when they are planning on returning to an area after an extended time away. However, many of these units become abandoned. When the renter defaults on their locker rent, the contents are put up for auction, usually bringing in a fraction of their actual worth. Often these units contain collectables and items held dear by seniors. When the senior downsizes, those things they can't fit in their smaller quarters are placed in storage. Upon their death, their children don't want to deal with the clutter and allow the unit to go unpaid, and so the problem is passed on to someone else.

As I pronounced judgement against the excesses of Western materialism, I felt God say, "Many of my people have received an abundance of blessings from me. I have poured gifts into them; I have blessed them with sound teaching, and I have equipped them with my weapons of warfare. My instructions are not put into practice, and the weapons I gave them grow rusty from disuse. And yet, my people crave more education, more conferences, more books, more training."

In case you were wondering what quote I discovered that day, here it is.

If you are feeling cluttered in your life, ask yourself the following question. "Do I have a spiritual closet full of boxes of spiritual gifts, treasures, insights and lessons that have been untouched and unused in years?" If the answer is yes, share these truths with others! Use them in your life today! Clear the closet!"

## Everything Else Pales in Comparison

*Suppose someone should offer me a plateful of crumbs after I had eaten a T-bone steak. I would say, "No, thank you. I am already satisfied." Christian, that is the secret - you can be so filled with the things of Christ, so enamored with the things of God that you do not have time for the sinful pleasures of the world.* - Billy Graham

I love this quote by Dr. Graham, as I, too, have realized that the things of heaven have caused the things of this world to pale in comparison. Don't misunderstand me, I have a deep appreciation for the beauty of the earth. I grew up close to the majestic Canadian Rockies and for me to breathe in the crisp mountain air is as satisfying as a steak dinner. I've sat on quiet tropical beaches and have been lulled into a peaceful sleep by the rhythm of the waves gently meeting the shore as surely as if God was singing a gentle lullaby to me.

I have been moved to tears by a symphony and I have been moved to dance by the joyful beat of a good band. I've laughed until my sides hurt with friends, and I have felt the comfort of the same friends during times of sorrow. I have happily sunk deep into the worlds created for me by an imaginative movie or a good book. I relish a thoughtful sermon or teaching that opens my mind and heart to new ways of looking at the world around me and God's kingdom.

However, I have grown dissatisfied with what the world offers. Television shows that might have appealed to me a few years ago now seem garish and off-kilter, as if the color on my television needs fine-tuning. Popular music and singers that once had an emotional pull now seem slightly manipulative and cloying. If you have ever taken a whiff of an inexpensive, counterfeit perfume after wearing the original scent for years, you'll understand what I mean.

C. S. Lewis describes this longing for *more* in his book,"*The Magician's Nephew*". Young Digory returns to the everyday world of his London row housing and races up to his mother's sickroom, carrying with him an apple that he took with permission from Aslan's garden. In Lewis' allegories, Aslan's garden and country represent the Kingdom of God.

*"There were of course all sorts of coloured things in the bedroom; the coloured counterpane on the bed, the wallpaper, the sunlight from the window, and Mother's pretty, pale blue dressing jacket. But the moment Digory took the Apple out of his pocket, all those things seemed to have scarcely any colour at all. Every one of them, even the*

*sunlight, looked faded and dingy. The brightness of the Apple threw strange lights on the ceiling. Nothing else was worth looking at: you couldn't look at anything else. And the smell of the Apple of Youth was as if there was a window in the room that opened on Heaven."* Lewis, C. S. *The Chronicles of Narnia: The Magician's Nephew.* New York: Harper Collins, 1955. Print

Have you been vaguely discontent as of late? Do the things that once brought you pleasure seem lifeless? Do the latest computer gadget, the latest video game, and the latest recording artist leave you wanting for more? Are you on the hunt for something new and exciting to fill that void? If you have been hungering and thirsting for more in your life, could I encourage you to satisfy your thirst on the living water of God? Nothing else can compare.

Isaiah 55:1-2 - *"Come, everyone who thirsts, come to the waters; and he who has no money, come, buy and eat! Come, buy wine and milk without money and without price. Why do you spend your money for that which is not bread, and your labor for that which does not satisfy. Listen diligently to me, and eat what is good, and delight yourselves in rich food."*

## *People Get Ready*

Are there areas in your life that God has asked you to get in order? Are you putting off paying overdue bills? Are your unessential purchases adding up to way beyond your financial means? Do you continue to spend even as your spirit feels God's conviction? Are you seeking to find self-worth through social status and prestige? Are there daily spiritual disciplines He is asking you to practice that you have been lax in pursuing? Do you hunger for a deeper, more intimate prayer life? Are you feeling God calling you back into fellowship with a supportive body of local believers? If so, you are not alone.

Our merciful, loving God is exhorting His people to gather spiritual provisions and to hone their skills of prayer and intercession. Many Christians sense urgent conviction when they fail to step out in obedience to His leading and direction. Many believers are experiencing an intensified longing to hear God's voice. Their hunger for His Word is insatiable, and they are spending copious amounts of time in Bible study, worship and quiet times. "Deep calls unto deep" and God is wooing His children closer to His heart as He desires to pour into them all that they will need in the coming days.

There are skills that cannot be learned in the heat of battle. These skills are vital and must be in our arsenal. Some of these skills require self-discipline if they are to be learned well. Hearing the word of the Lord, discerning deception and stepping past fear into obedience require courage. Cultivating the courage needed to stay still until the Lord directs you to move will give you the ability to remain in His peace when the world is shaken.

God remains committed to His children. Throughout the ages, He lovingly gave His people warnings of what was to come, and His promises have remained true. His character has not changed; His plans and purposes, hopes and dreams for His children have not changed either. He is forever faithful and in His graciousness, He urges us to be proactive and to prepare to the best of our ability for what lies ahead.

## Stirring Up a Hornet's Nest

A friend invested time and energy in creating a beautiful backyard. Over the years, she gathered a charming, eclectic collection of outdoor furniture that she artfully arranged underneath majestic, mature trees. She kept perfectly manicured lawns and grew spectacular flower beds. As a finishing touch, she built an attractive privacy fence with the help of good friends.

The enticing, sweet sound of birds chirping outside her bedroom window woke her every morning, and she would longingly gaze out the patio window at the beauty of her little oasis from her breakfast table each day. Longingly gaze, you ask? Yes, longingly. Unfortunately, her backyard had been taken over by flying bullies that had made their home in the eaves troughs just above her back door. In order for her to walk out into her sanctuary, she had to pass by the hornet's nest. As the nest grew, she spent less and less time in her backyard.

She attempted to deal with the hornets' nest on her own. She used a variety of pesticide sprays recommended by her local home centre; she surveyed her friends for folk remedies, and she prayed. One night, she risked life and limb by lashing out at the nest with a broom handle. The nest did not budge, and the pests' reign remained. The hornets appeared to be more aggressive as a result of her failed counterattack. My friend continued to live in exile from her kingdom.

After a few weeks, her once-immaculate lawn began to look rough around the edges. She didn't mow it as often. Each week on the eve of garbage day, she would wait until late evening when she knew the hornets would be asleep.. She would then race across the lawn so she could place her garbage cans in the back lane. She no longer invited her friends to gather around her fire pit. The constant buzz of hornets outside her window became as annoying as her alarm clock.

One of her friends offered to deal with the hornets. Knowledgeable in pest control; he had successfully removed many nests. Although she was afraid of stirring up the hornet's nest, she chose to push past her fear and trust her friend. Her trust was rewarded. With grim satisfaction, she watched from the safety of her kitchen as the hornets were vanquished, and their nest was carried away for safe disposal.

My friend chose wisely. She could have remained paralyzed by her fear, intimidated by the hornets. She could have continued to modify her lifestyle, by becoming an exile from her back yard as the hornets' nest continued to grow. She could have abandoned her backyard entirely and began anew by working on her front yard. Instead, she admitted that she was powerless over those hornets and surrendered control to an expert who had her best interests at heart.

Is there a situation in your life that has spun out of control? Do you feel bullied by the enemy? Have you rearranged your life to ensure you won't have to confront the problem directly? Have you come to a place where you realize that ignoring the problem won't solve it? Perhaps it's time that you take that problem to the greatest expert of all. I'm sure that He has the perfect solution if you have ears to listen.

## God's Ambassadors

Although we live in earthly bodies, we represent a heavenly kingdom. You might say that we bring Heaven to Earth. God might send you as His spokesperson to your workplace or your classroom. Your assignment might find you in the grocery store behind an anxious mama with an overtired toddler. You might be sent an emergency directive from the Commander-in-Chief as you sit beside a fellow patient in your doctor's waiting room or while standing at a bus stop. You could be commissioned as His representative of grace during rush-hour traffic on a busy highway.

Unlike earthly ambassadors, we are called to spend most of our lives outside the walls of our secure embassies. We carry out our official duties in the highways and byways of the land God has assigned to us. Unlike earthly diplomats, the words we carry are not meant for the ears of the rich and powerful alone. Earthly diplomats often abuse their rights to diplomatic immunity, as God's ambassadors, we are held to a higher standard. We are living, breathing testaments of the founding principles of the Kingdom we represent.

2 Corinthians 3:2-3 (MSG) - *"Your very lives are a letter that anyone can read by just looking at you. Christ himself wrote it—not with ink, but with God's living Spirit; not chiseled into stone, but carved into human lives."*

We have been given our orders; may we walk them out in ways that will bring honour to God's kingdom.

## Can't Get a Word in Edgewise?

Feeling a little unheard lately? God feels your pain!

Sally met Mary through the glowing recommendation of a mutual acquaintance that found Mary to be a compassionate, intelligent, and trustworthy friend with much wisdom, charm and devotion. She knew Mary's friendship would bless Sally. As the two new friends worked in the same building, they found themselves meeting several times for lunch.

It was the norm for Sally's meal to sit nearly untouched as her fork was used more times than not as a gesturing device to emphasize key points to her many stories. On the other hand, Mary made steady progress through her salad, entree, and dessert, having tried and failed to interject her own thoughts into Sally's free flow of anecdotes and retelling of her woes. Mary made valiant attempts to get a word in edgewise but rarely saw much success.

On one such occasion, Mary pushed away her empty plate and reached for her coffee cup. Sally glanced over at her dining companion in surprise. "Oh dear, I'm such a slow eater!" With a wry chuckle of amusement, Mary merely nodded as Sally looked at her watch and called their waiter over for the bill and a doggie bag. "It was such a great visit, and we must do this again sometime!" exclaimed Sally. After a quick hug, she headed back to work.

If she were honest, Sally would admit she left these lunch dates with a vague sense of emptiness and disappointment. She couldn't understand why her relationship with Mary lacked the closeness and intimacy that had been spoken of by their mutual friend.

Some Christians find prayer difficult and unfulfilling. They complain that although they storm the heavens day after day, praying fervently for their loved ones and the world around them, they fail to see many answers to their prayers. These disheartened Christians struggle with feelings of jealousy and envy when others speak of their intimate relationship with God. When they hear glowing testimonies of God's direct guidance and intervention in answer to specific prayer, they feel left out. "Maybe God loves them more, maybe God really does have favourites, maybe they have an inside track. They are more spiritual than me. Maybe I just wasn't cut out to be someone with whom God would consider worthy of His time."

Perhaps, these Christians have forgotten the art of two-sided communication. Prayer is a dialogue between God and man. In their haste to have their petitions heard and their needs met, they failed to sit quietly, in a place of active listening, waiting for God's answer.

Learning to hear the voice of God requires time, patience, and faith. God is eager and willing to speak to us at any time through His word and the wise counsel of mature believers. He waits for us to draw away with Him as He often speaks to us during times of personal devotion. If you allow Him to get a word in edgewise, you'll find those choice nuggets of wisdom and life-giving truth to are so satisfying that you'll find yourself asking Him to take over the conversation.

## *Getting Out of the Way*

I am fiercely loyal, and I have the tenacity of a bulldog when I feel it necessary to go to war for a loved one. If they are knocked down by abuse, slander, or mistreatment, watch out! I will do everything in my power to stand between them and those who might want to cause them harm. If anyone dares to speak negatively about a friend in my hearing, they will be met with a cold, icy glare. When a fellow believer brings a complaint about someone else to me, and I discover they failed first to approach the person in question, I pull out one of my favourite Bible passages.

Matthew 18:15-16 - *"If your brother sins against you, go and tell him his fault, between you and him alone. If he listens to you, you have gained your brother. But if he does not listen, take one or two others along with you, that every charge may be established by the evidence of two or three witnesses."*

Fidelity is a fine character trait to nurture. However, excessive protectiveness creates a dangerous hazard to those I love. Much like a watchful dog who keeps emergency medical technicians at bay as he stands guard over his injured owner, my overprotectiveness hinders those with greater expertise from doing their job. Long ago, I surrendered this area of my life to the Lord, and I hold myself accountable to trusted friends, giving them permission to challenge me if they see these unhealthy patterns resurface.

God is in control, and He knows what He is doing in the lives of those I love. As I intercede for those in crisis, I surrender my concerns about the situation. God knows best, and He will dispatch those best suited for the job at hand. There are times when God calls me forward as one of his healing agents, and there are times He calls me to stand still. Both scenarios require that I recognize His voice, and both scenarios require that I give Him my instant obedience and complete trust.

2 Chronicles 20:17 - *"You will not need to fight in this battle. Stand firm, hold your position, and see the salvation of the Lord on your behalf, O Judah and Jerusalem. Do not be afraid and do not be dismayed. Tomorrow go out against them, and the Lord will be with you."*

## *My Times Are in His Hands*

Isaiah 28:16 - *"Whoever believes will not be in haste."*

*"Whoever believes won't get rattled or hustled; he won't let time get on top of him or dictate to him. Don't we wish were true of ourselves? Time, the enemy... How often do you hear people saying, – how often do you hear yourself saying, "Oh, I haven't got time!" I haven't got time... No, we haven't, for time has got us, or most of us."* Evelyn Underhill, *"The Mastery of Time"*

Psalm 31:14-15a - *"But I trust in you, O Lord; I say, 'You are my God.' My times are in your hand."*

Daylight Savings Time had ended, and it was time to fall back. As I reset the many clocks in my apartment, David's words popped into my mind. "My times are in His Hands." I laughed outloud. By all accounts, my times were not in His hands, nor in mine! My clock radio was set a half hour ahead. I had heard somewhere that this would get me out of bed at the first buzz. Unfortunately, I hit my snooze bar just as often. The clock on my microwave kept its own pace and needed to be reset back to the correct time at least once a week. My boombox's clock ran five minutes slow. My cell phone refused to acknowledge the passing of Daylight Savings Time. My DVD player pointedly ignored the changing of the seasons. As I walked through my small apartment, it appeared that I lived in many time zones. I could only rely on the accuracy of my computer's clock.

Even with such an embarrassment of riches, I was always running out of time.

At the end of too many days, I come to the sad realization that time just slipped away. While I proclaim my time is in God's hands; it rarely is. I seldom ask the Lord how He would like me to spend each day. By neglecting to consult with Him, I renege on the promise I made when I surrendered my life to Him. The use of my time was included in our covenant. If I am a bondservant of Jesus Christ, the 8760 hours He entrusts to me each year are not my own to manage or mismanage as I please.

As God's bondservant, I submit my calendar and schedule for His approval. My day-planner is His to rearrange as He sees fit, for my own benefit and the benefit of those God would call me to serve. Time is no longer my master.

## FLEE THE TYRANNY OF IMMEDIACY

Ecclesiastes 3:11 - *"He has made everything beautiful in its time. Also, he has put eternity into man's heart, yet so that he cannot find out what God has done from the beginning to the end."*

Pregnant women wait for the day when their children are born. As the days and months of their pregnancies progress, and their bellies grow, they find themselves talking to the newborn within, longing for the day when they can meet the mysterious new life growing inside them. They envision counting little toes and fingers, stroking soft rose-petal cheeks and snuggling their newborns in their arms. Yet, if you were to talk to a mother whose premature child is in a neonatal intensive-care unit, she would lament, "If only my baby would have stayed safe within me, even one more week, even one more day. It wasn't the right time yet."

We have little opportunity to learn the discipline of patience in today's world of rapid-fire email and instant downloads. If a website takes longer than three seconds to load, most Internet surfers move on to the next site. You no longer have to stand in line at a movie theatre; you can buy your ticket in advance. If a friend doesn't respond to your text right away, you wonder if they are angry with you. Jetliners now travel around the world in less than a day.

The notion of trusting God to fulfill His promises in His time is foreign to those who have grown up in the age of all things instant. However, to see God's perfect will executed at just the right time requires not only patience but trust. It demands that we submit our agendas and calendars into the hands of the One who knows our future and who holds all time in His hands. Our divine midwife knows the exact hour and moment His promises are ready to be birthed into life.

*"He may delay because it would not be safe to give us at once what we ask: we are not ready for it. To give before we could truly receive, would be to destroy the very heart and hope of prayer, to cease to be our Father. The delay itself may work to bring us nearer to our help, to increase the desire, perfect the prayer, and ripen the receptive condition."* MacDonald, George, and Rolland Hein. *Creation in Christ: Unspoken Sermons*. Vancouver: Regent College Pub., 2004. Print.

## WHEN THE WORLD'S ALL THAT IT SHOULD BE

Spring had arrived, and a balmy fortnight melted any remaining snowdrifts and caused the underlying snow mould to dry up and blow away in the gentle breeze. I took advantage of the pleasant weather one morning to do a little shopping in my neighbourhood. As my neighbours were not bundled from head to foot in bulky winter gear, they were easy to recognize and we exchanged friendly smiles as they hurried along their way on their own errands. It seemed the whole neighbourhood was enjoying the weather. Later that day, I luxuriated in the soothing warmth of the sun on my back as I sat on my balcony. I even enjoyed a cold drink as I peered down at golfers far below at the nearby golf course.

The next morning, a fresh blanket of snow covered the landscape. Although I had turned up the heat in my apartment overnight, I still shivered. My cold hands sought out the warmth that radiated from my morning cup of coffee as I spotted a few bundled up pedestrians huddled in a bus shelter in hopes of escaping the biting wind. With a heavy sigh, I turned from the dreary scene to pull on my winter coat. It was Sunday morning, and it was time to brave the elements as I headed out to church. As I walked out my door, I found myself singing:

*Blessed be Your Name*
   *When the sun's shining down on me*
   *When the world's 'all as it should be'*
   *Blessed be Your Name*

*Blessed be Your Name*
   *On the road marked with suffering*
   *Though there's pain in the offering*
   *Blessed be Your Name*

© 2001 Matt Redman
   Album: *Where Angels Fear To Tread* (2002)

If your spring has temporarily turned back to winter, bless His Name! Seasons will pass, even the most painful ones, but His love endures forever.

## *Walking In Obedience*

In December of 1983, I sought the Lord's direction as to where I should go after finishing an advanced training course at Youth With A Mission. My inclination was to join an international outreach targeting the 1984 Los Angeles summer Olympic games. I had heard remarkable accounts from previous Olympic outreaches, and I wanted a part of the action. With an extension on my visa that allowed me to stay in the United States for a few more months and the necessary finances in place, I felt confident that I was heading to California.

However, God appeared to have other plans. My leadership asked me to serve in a refugee camp along the border of Thailand and Cambodia. The mission team urgently needed people with my particular skill set. Reluctantly, I said I would take their request before the Lord, and I immediately felt His leading. I arranged my plane tickets, visas, and other travel arrangements in short order, albeit with a heavy heart. As I prepared to go, I asked the Lord for a Bible verse or personal word of encouragement that I could take with me as confirmation.

One morning during my regular quiet time, I was drawn to an obscure Bible verse:

I Samuel 17:17-18 - *"And Jesse said to David his son, '"Take for your brothers an ephah of this parched grain, and these ten loaves, and carry them quickly to the camp to your brothers. Also take these ten cheeses to the commander of their thousand. See if your brothers are well, and bring some token from them."*

Huh? What sort of scripture was that?

Another morning in prayer, a picture of an old Asian woman flashed in my mind. She stood just inside a simple hut wearing a faded saffron-coloured blouse and a dark purple sarong. She carried something on her head, wrapped up in cloth woven in a plaid design of rich purple, blue and red.

Huh? What sort of picture was that?

I had no emotional connection with refugees or Thailand, and I was still pouting over the fact that I was missing the party in Los Angeles even as I wrote the team to say I was coming.

Two months later, a fellow YWAMer picked me up at the Bangkok International Airport. As he drove through the windy crowded city streets like a maniac, he grilled me on my life. His first question was an obvious one as he asked where I was from. I answered that I was formerly from Calgary, Alberta. His eyebrows shot up. "Hey, I suppose you don't know Brenda, do you?"

My eyebrows shot up in response. Brenda was one of my dearest friends, my sister in countless ways, and I had lost contact with her. We were travelling so much that our mail hadn't caught up with us. He chattered on, apparently unaware of the countless near misses we had with motorcycles and old pickup trucks that appeared to be hell-bent on playing 'chicken' with our massive van.

"She'll be working in the same camp as you." He paused as he had to manoeuvre around a huge pothole. "Oh, and she'll be living across the street from you, I can tell you that she'll be happy to see you as she's missing home." Suddenly, the verse from Samuel made sense. I was bringing refreshment to my sister. A whisper of a positive emotion barely rustled within me. I was still there by obedience alone.

When I arrived in the town where I would live, I had a joyful reunion with Brenda that caught her off-guard and almost caused her to faint, but that's another story. I felt a few more rustlings of positive emotions stir within me.

A few days later, we drove through open gates into the refugee camp. I glanced around the world where I'd be working. Bamboo huts, dirt roads, open sewage, women wandering around in brightly coloured blouses tucked into sarongs, men on bicycles and multitudes of children running alongside our truck overwhelmed my senses.

Then I saw her. The very woman I saw in the flash of a vision two months earlier. She was wearing a faded saffron-coloured blouse and a dark purple sarong. She carried a bundle of rice on her head, wrapped in the purple, blue and red plaid cloth I had seen in the vision. I later discovered the cloth had multiple uses. It could be used as a skirt for a woman or a makeshift towel for men as they walked home from the community showers, but usually they were used as carry-alls.

I knew at that moment that my step of obedience and sacrifice had a purpose. I immediately felt the emotional confirmation I had been seeking months earlier. The Cambodian people captured my heart. The Olympic games came and went, but I didn't give them another thought.

Shortly after my return to Canada after a year in Thailand, my family and I went to see "The Killing Fields." The movie exposed the horrors suffered by the Cambodian people under the ruthless Khmer Rouge. It's last scenes were filmed in the camp where I worked. Actual refugees from the camp served as extras. Oh, and one of those extras? You guessed it! The same woman from my vision wandered across the screen, wearing the same outfit and carrying the same load. My cousin firmly placed his hand on my shoulder to stop me from rising to my feet as I was so excited to see my people again.

Perhaps you had a heart desire that you set aside to follow God's plan. Trust God that as you step out in obedience, He will run to meet you. Trust Him to transplant His heart into yours. Ask Him, and He will show you why He chose you to be His ambassador. He will give you a strategy to be His hands, His feet and His voice in the place He has planted you.

## HIS KINDNESS LEADS TO REPENTANCE

My heart grieves when people declare that natural disasters, man-made catastrophes, wars, and acts of terror are God's punishments or His judgments over nations and regions. In the same breath, these pundits speak of a coming revival and a new harvest of believers who will be drawn to the Lord because of these horrific disasters.

I did not come to the Lord out of a fear of His punishment; I came because of His kindness and forgiveness. I approached Him because I realized my life was not working; I realized I had messed things up so badly that there was no way I could fix things. I was drawn to the cross by His promise to take my broken life and make something beautiful of it if I would give it into His hands.

Although I grew up in church, I had little understanding of what sin was. Sin was something murderers, thieves, bullies, and rogues did. Of course, I knew the sting of conviction when I did something wrong, but I honestly didn't think I was that bad compared to the terrible sinners out there. And yet, God still wooed me to His throne by revealing His grace. It was only after He captured my sinful, selfish heart that He began to deal with those areas of my life that did not line up with His word. Most Christians I know surrendered to the Lord in similar circumstances.

I have walked with the Lord for over 35 years, and I only know a small handful of Christians who came to the Lord because of a fear of hell or a fear of God's angry hand. I haven't met anyone who came to the Lord because their house blew down or because God destroyed their city. If you polled most unsaved people, they would say they wouldn't go anywhere near a harsh, angry God who doles out wrath and punishment by destroying their lives. I don't blame them; I tend to run in the opposite direction from angry, wrathful people, even if they are yelling at me that they are the only ones who can save me. Police officers and first responders are well aware of this phenomenon and are trained to approach those they are trying to rescue in such a way that would not cause them to run and hide.

I worked with refugees who escaped horrific brutalities inflicted upon them by their countrymen. Many survived natural disasters, floods, and monsoons. Those who came to the Lord during those harsh times came to Him through those who modelled God's unselfish love, mercy, generosity, and forgiveness. The refugees who had become believers before the horrors fell on their land were the ones who felt the conviction of the Lord. They repented for not reaching out to their neighbours with the true gospel. They repented of idolatry and their presumption that bad things never happened to good people. God's conviction only came after they were in a place of safety, far away from the horrors they endured. During seasons of significant loss of loved ones, homes and livelihoods, they only felt the sustaining grace, comfort, and strength of the Lord as He carried them through.

*It's your kindness that leads to repentance*
*It's your blood that brings forgiveness*
*It's your mercy that leads me here*
*To your throne of grace*

*In your kindness I find repentance*
*In your blood I find forgiveness*
*In your mercy I find myself*
*At Your throne of grace, Your throne of grace*

Copyright © John Barnett
1991 Mercy/Vineyard Publishing

## *My God is Not Stone-Faced*

I loved visiting my parent's friends who were farmers when I was a child. I remember the scent of warm hay in the barn as I searched for baby kittens. I remember the crisp sound of beans being snapped into earthen bowls as my mother and unofficial aunties sat on the front porch of the old farmhouse in the late afternoon to escape the heat of the kitchen. Any children on the porch were charged with the task of watching for distant dust clouds caused by the packed pick-up trucks returning from a day in the field. Even before the trucks turned into the long driveway up to the house, a cooler of frosty drinks waited for the thirsty workers.

The men swapped stories as they sprawled out on the old broken-down couches that lined the covered porch. The farmers' weather-beaten, taciturn faces fascinated me. With little emotion, the adults spoke of the hard decisions that they made each day to keep their farms afloat. Heifers and steers that their children had raised from calves would be sent to auction each year. Parcels of land that had been in their family for generations were sometimes sold during hard times. They'd brush off fatigue, injuries, crushing disappointments, and personal betrayals by family members with the same disinterest as they'd give a fly they flicked off a shirt sleeve. They had learned to keep their emotions in check. As they aged, they guarded their thoughts and feelings even more.

I became more observant as I grew and discovered a few chinks in their armour that revealed tender hearts. Those tiny cracks were not exposed by the wearing down of their inner strength by the hard knocks and setbacks that were part of being a farmer. No, those cracks were the result of the loving assault against the walls of their heart. It was hard to resist the outstretched arms of a sweet grandchild when they ran toward their grandfather. That child knew they'd be tossed high up into the air, and they'd make their grandfather smile. Children have a way of wiggling past the armour adults place around their hearts.

Many see God as a distant Creator, cold and disinterested. God is the very opposite of the closed-hearted Patriarch they presume Him to be. From the time of Adam, God chose to keep His heart open to His children. Our disappointing behaviour, rebellion, and rejection cost Him dearly, yet it did not weaken His resolve. Instead of building self-protecting walls of separation that would shield Him from further pain, He decided to build a bridge through the blood of His only Son. He does not hide His heart from humanity, quite the contrary! God wears His heart on His sleeve. He waits with open arms to swoop us up into His embrace.

## The Promised Land is Occupied

*Deuteronomy 7:1-10*

I have a friend who is a newcomer to Canada. Although she is thankful for God's favour that opened doors for her small family to resettle here, the move has not been an easy adjustment for her. As she is aware that I worked with refugees for many years, our conversations often drift toward the joys and struggles of adapting to a new land.

Like most refugees, she fled her homeland in a panic, carrying only the barest of necessities. Although just out of her teens herself, she was thrust into the role of guardian over her younger sister. Her nation's civil war separated the pair from the rest of their family. The Lord's protection was over them, and the sisters found themselves in the relative safety of a refugee camp. There, they faced inadequate food, poor sanitation, language barriers, loneliness, and culture shock.

They applied for resettlement in Canada, even as they hoped they could return to their beloved country. It was difficult to fight against the debilitating depression and lethargy that is widespread in most refugee camps. She endured countless resettlement interviews with many nations, none of which promised much hope. There were no signs of a truce in her home country. After several months of sleepless nights spent in prayer, she was granted permission to enter Canada along with her sister. Less than a year after receiving permission, they reached their new home.

Much like the children of Israel, she discovered her promised land was already inhabited and that she would have wage battle to take the land the Lord had set before her. Unlike the flesh and blood enemies of the Israelites, the foes that faced my friend were not visible to the naked eye. These enemies were just as dangerous as those that opposed the Israelites so long ago.

In her first years in Canada, discouragement, disappointment, and loneliness were her constant enemies. She knew she had to lean on God for understanding. She couldn't grasp the culture of her new country. A humble heart was her only defence against a critical spirit as she resisted judgments against a nation she did not yet understand. She learned the hard truth that choosing to have a grateful heart must be a deliberate and conscious choice if she were to prosper.

If you find yourself in a strange land, a land that you would not have chosen for yourself, you have a choice. Perhaps you face serious health issues. Perhaps you are struggling in an unhappy marriage; perhaps your children have fallen into addictions. You have a decision to make. You can choose to serve the giants of your land - Bitterness, Criticism, Doubt, Hopelessness, and Ungratefulness, or you can choose to serve the Lord.

Joshua 24:15 - *"...And if it is evil in your eyes to serve the Lord, choose this day whom you will serve, whether the gods your fathers served in the region beyond the River, or the gods of the Amorites in whose land you dwell. But as for me and my house, we will serve the Lord."*

## Now That I Have Your Attention

I have never been a morning person, a fact to which my friends and family readily attest. However, I'm definitely not one of those people whose loved ones need to place a mug of coffee in easy reach, and then back away slowly with one eye on the nearest exit. My problem with mornings is best explained by the absence of cognitive thought and a lack of awareness of my surroundings.

As a child, I needed my mother to guide me along in the morning. Although she was busy overseeing all five of her children as they prepared for school, she knew that her eldest daughter needed a little extra prompting each day. I would sit on the edge of my bed as I faced the task of getting dressed. My mother would call up the stairs, "Put on your left sock, Katherine!" Obediently, I would put on the sock and after a few moments, my mother would call up again. "Now put on the right sock." I would comply.

Even the family dog understood I needed a bit of a push and a shove and would alert me by a polite whine when it was time for breakfast. It wasn't unusual for my mother to send me back upstairs to turn my shirt the right way around and to put on matching socks after a quick inspection. As the morning progressed, I became more aware of the world around me. "Cream of Wheat for breakfast, my favourite! Now how did I get down here?" I was never late for school although I often had no idea how I arrived in my classroom.

I still need about ninety minutes after my alarm clock rings to come to a full realization that there is a world around me. Most of my acquaintances know to give me that time before expecting me to carry on a meaningful conversation. If they have something important to discuss with me, they first ask how long I've been awake before continuing. Even God understands; after all, He created me.

As a new believer, I struggled with self-condemnation. I had been taught that if you did not have morning quiet times, you were grieving the Holy Spirit. I had the quiet aspect of morning devotions down to a fine science, but the devotional aspect was sorely lacking. It took the Lord a while to convince me that He'd much rather have my undivided attention in the late evening than my mindless adherence to the law in the morning. God understood me and gave me more grace than I gave myself.

One autumn morning, the Lord reminded me of His grace as I

sat on a bench outside my apartment waiting for a friend. I was vaguely aware of the blue sky and sunlight. I saw traffic going by, and I was aware of people coming and going, but I was not fully awake. I was in my usual morning fog.

A feminine gasp of joy brought me out of whatever daydream I was having, and I looked around, trying to find the source of the gasp. I spotted a young couple that stood stopped a few feet away from me. As they were foreign students, I couldn't understand the young girl's excited conversation with her boyfriend, but I followed her gaze across the street to a majestic tree in full fall foliage. Vibrant yellows and browns adorned every branch. It was breathtaking. The couple pulled out their cell phones and took a couple of pictures, then hurried on their way. I looked up to the heavens and gave the Creator His due, then gazed at His masterpiece again.

In the next heartbeat, a mighty gust of wind shook the tree, causing almost every leaf to fall to the ground. I smiled as I watched the leaves swirl and dance merrily down the sidewalk. I was glad I had caught the moment. I sensed God's chuckle as He whispered to my heart, "Good morning, Katherine. I'm glad you enjoyed my gift and now that you are awake, have a great day."

## *Is It Time to Let Go of Your Night Light?*

"Peek-a-boo! I see you!" Anyone who has entertained a baby knows that this old stand-by is a perennial favourite. Kids love the suspense. Will mommy's face appear behind those hands? Will daddy pop up from behind the chair? In an infant's mind, out-of-sight means 'Mama's not there, and I don't know if she is really coming back!' What they cannot see with their eyes does not exist. In the middle of the night, a baby doesn't find much comfort in Papa's voice reassuring them from down the hall. They need his touch, and they need his husky sleep-deprived whisper in their ear to be truly soothed.

As a well-adjusted child develops past toddlerhood into preschool years, he learns to play independently, and he doesn't always need to have his parents in his sight to be at peace. A reassuring word from the kitchen as he plays in the living room is often all he needs as his mother prepares supper. The sound of his father's voice over the phone is enough to tide him over until he can snuggle in his papa's arms at the end of the day.

However, many children go through a phase of being afraid of the dark and want a night light for them to feel secure enough to sleep. A wise parent does not allow the child to dwell on this fear for long and weans their child from the need for a night light as soon as possible. Often, this requires the parent to stay in a darkened bedroom as their child drifts off to sleep. They allow only their physical presence to act as the child's comfort. A child must learn to trust that his papa is there even when he cannot see his papa's face or hear his papa's voice.

Many Christians regress to childish behaviour when they face times of darkness and uncertainty. They doubt God's love for them when they cannot see His face or hear His voice. Some even begin to doubt God's existence when the 'dark night of the soul' extends for too long. Much like a little child, they foolishly believe that darkness causes their Heavenly Papa to disappear from their presence. They demand the 'night light' to be turned on so they can see their Heavenly Father and be reassured that He is indeed there. God hopes His children will move past such infantile reasoning. He longs that we take Him at His word.

Isaiah 49: 14-15 - *But Zion said, "The Lord has forsaken me; my Lord has forgotten me." "Can a woman forget her nursing child, that she should have no compassion on the son of her womb? Even these may forget, yet I will not forget you."*

God's ability to draw near to us is not contingent on our ability to sense that He is near. There is no power on heaven or earth that can separate us from His love.

Psalm 139: 7-12 - *"Where shall I go from your Spirit? Or where shall I flee from your presence? If I ascend to heaven, you are there! If I make my bed in Sheol, you are there! If I take the wings of the morning and dwell in the uttermost parts of the sea, even there your hand shall lead me, and your right hand shall hold me. If I say, "Surely the darkness shall cover me, and the light about me be night," even the darkness is not dark to you; the night is bright as the day, for darkness is as light with you."*

## Free Fall

One day, a young man decided to take a hike in the mountains. Planning to camp, he carried an overstuffed backpack. As the afternoon turned into dusk, he stood on the edge of a cliff to watch the setting sun. Stumbling, he found himself tumbling down into the ravine. Desperately reaching out, the hapless hiker managed to grab a branch growing out of the side of the cliff. Knowing that he could not hold on for long, he screamed into the darkness, "Help! Help! Is anyone out there?" The weight of his backpack threatened to send him toppling backwards, and as he was clinging to the branch with both hands, he was unable to remove the pack.

With a crack of thunder, a deep voice filled the night air. "I can save you!" The man looked around, but he couldn't see anyone. Confused, he asked, "Who is this?" The voice replied, "This is God." Taken aback, the man asked, "Can you help me?" "Yes," God answered. "Let go of the branch. I will catch you" The man was silent for a time as he considered God's suggestion. Clinging even tighter to the weakening limb, he called out again, "Is there anyone else out there?"

In times of crisis, it is natural to grasp the first thing we can grab onto and hold on fast. Like the man in this old tale, we usually place our trust in something or someone who will eventually fail as our flimsy handhold was never designed to bear the full weight of our burden for long. In our blind panic, we set aside rationality and blindly ignore the tell-tell signs that our makeshift supports are beginning to crumble.

God asks us to do an awkward thing at such times. In his wisdom, He knows that our branch will fail us eventually, and we will tumble down into the abyss. He answers our timid plea, "Is there anyone else there?" with a simple request. "Let go." God knows that He is more than able to catch us and carry us, no matter how heavy the weight we carry upon our shoulders.

Is it time for you to let go of the spindly branch on which you have inappropriately placed your trust and put that trust in the One whose promises will never fail?

## *To Every Season...*

Ecclesiastes 3:1 – *"For everything there is a season, and a time for every matter under heaven."*

Everyone has a favourite season. Some enjoy the freshness of spring; others can't wait to bask in the sun-drenched days of summer. Hearty sports enthusiasts can't wait for winter, preparing their snowboards and skis in anticipation of the first snowfall.

Autumn is my favourite season. I love the warm days and crisp nights. I feast my eyes on the ambers and golds of the fall foliage that provide a protective canopy over the neighbourhood flower gardens that are still in full bloom throughout most of September.

As a Canadian missionary, I was homesick for the four seasons when I lived in the subtropical climates of Asia, South America, and Hawaii. I have always treasured the distinct seasons in my native land, even the snowy winter with all its hazards.

I have been in fiery debates with friends as we extolled the virtues of winter, spring, summer, and fall. Most Canadians are fiercely loyal to their particular season of choice, and the weather plays a significant role in our daily conversation. Spring-lovers can't understand why anyone would find winter anything but bitterly cruel; winter-lovers look upon summer-lovers as wimps. At the end of the day, Canadians thrive in all seasons despite our good-natured grumblings. We have no other choice but to adapt!

Although not quite as distinct, there are seasons in the life of a healthy church as well. There are seasons when praise and celebration are in the forefront, and exuberant worshippers relish every Sunday service. During such times, those who love systematic Bible study and meaty sermons might shake their heads at what they secretly consider fluff and show. When the church body moves toward new expressions of community service and outreach, some within the body complain of an apparent lack of pastoral care toward those already in the congregation.

In the same way that God provided the four seasons to bring balance and fruitfulness to our natural world, so the Holy Spirit desires to bring a supernatural ebb and flow within a body of believers. We do a great disservice to Him and those around us by grumbling when our local body enters a season to which we, as individuals, would not naturally gravitate. By stubbornly refusing to budge from our comfort zone, we lose the opportunity to become rounded and balanced in our personal walk with the Lord.

Let us gratefully embrace the season in which we live today!

Isaiah 55:10-11 - *"For as the rain and the snow come down from heaven and do not return there but water the earth, making it bring forth and sprout, giving seed to the sower and bread to the eater, so shall my word be that goes out from my mouth; it shall not return to me empty, but it shall accomplish that which I purpose, and shall succeed in the thing for which I sent it."*

## The Fog Will Lift

1 Corinthians 13:12 (MSG) – *"We don't yet see things clearly. We're squinting in a fog, peering through a mist. But it won't be long before the weather clears and the sun shines bright! We'll see it all then, see it all as clearly as God sees us, knowing him directly just as He knows us!"*

Shortly after dawn one fall morning, I opened my blinds to enjoy the view. A glorious sunrise shone across the river valley that wound its way through my city. I marvelled at the fall foliage; so many trees had changed colour overnight. Satisfied and grateful, I turned away from the window and continued my established morning routine: breakfast, coffee, then checking my email. Not necessarily in that order!

After about an hour of answering emails and checking out my various ministry sites, I reached for my insulated coffee mug on my desk. As it wasn't in its usual place, I needed to pull my attention away from my computer screen and back to my desk as I searched for the mug. It's amazing what a difference a few inches can make. I put the cup back where it belonged. As I did, I happened to glance out my window. I was shocked! I could barely see across the street.

A heavy fog had rolled in while my morning business had kept me occupied. Even as I gazed out the window, the fog thickened, further restricting my view. It effectively blocked my ability to see anything beyond a few feet past my balcony. I felt claustrophobic and isolated. I knew the sun was shining above the fog although I could barely discern its thin, silvery reflection through the grey mist. I needed to be patient; the bright morning rays would eventually burn off the haze that obscured my vision. I had no doubt I'd see the sun again. About a half-hour later, I whispered a prayer of thankfulness. My view had returned.

That day turned out to be a glorious autumn day. A bright blue sky accented the vibrant reds, oranges, and russet landscape filling the river valley below. As I looked across the horizon, I felt I could see forever.

Perhaps you are in a spiritual fog. Where you once saw clearly, you now find it hard to discern His plans and purposes in your life. Perhaps you feel hemmed in on every side. Perhaps worries and responsibilities press against you, hindering your ability to see past the burdens of the moment. Be encouraged with this truth. Although your immediate circumstances darken your horizon, the Lord's light is still there. Your vision might be obscured by the mist of self-doubt, fear, or confusion. Be of good cheer for God is still there. He hasn't vanished. Trust Him. As surely as the sun rises, the clouds will lift. Spiritual fog cannot withstand the warmth of the Son.

Isaiah 60: 1-3 – *"Arise, shine, for your light has come, and the glory of the Lord has risen upon you. For behold, darkness shall cover the earth, and thick darkness the peoples; but the Lord will arise upon you, and His glory will be seen upon you. And nations shall come to your light, and kings to the brightness of your rising."*

## *I Told You Twice, Isn't That Enough?*

A man sits at the dining room table, waiting for his dinner to appear. From his vantage, he spies his wife stomping around in the kitchen, slamming pots in the sink, and violently spooning food onto plates. As his dish is placed before him, it rattles from the force that was used to set it down. His wife pours a mug of coffee then slams it down with equal force. As she sits across the table from him, her baleful stare never falters. The tension is palatable, making the meal very unpalatable. Finally, he garners up the courage to look across the table and ask. "Is there anything wrong, dear?"

His wife dramatically lifts her hand, raises one finger and points to the wall calendar. A fluorescent red heart marks the current date with the single letter "A" in its centre. "You missed our anniversary again. You didn't even give me a card. How could you? I cooked you your favourite meal and wore a beautiful dress just for you. Forty years we've been married, and you never tell me you love me. I've had it up to here! I want a divorce!"

Bewildered, her husband protests. "But, I told you I loved you the day I asked you to marry me, I told you again for good measure the day we were wed. I figured if I had changed my mind; I'd have let you know."

This joke came to mind during a time of worship one Sunday morning. I was tired; I was in pain, and my mind was wandering. I was distracted by anything that crossed my vision: a sweet little girl in her father's arms, a young couple that were newly engaged. A noisy two-year-old was having a major meltdown. I noticed a friend who I hadn't seen in months enter the sanctuary and couldn't wait until the service ended so we could catch up on each other's news. I wrinkled my nose in disgust at a wad of gum on the bottom of the chair in front of me. All the while, I sang along with the rest of the congregation.

I heard a wee small voice deep inside my heart. It appeared my lack of focus had caught God's attention. I didn't sense His anger; if anything, I sensed a wry amusement in His tone. "Excuse me, I hate to interrupt your thoughts but isn't this about you and Me? Remember Me? That's me who you are singing about. I'm right here!" There wasn't a whiff of passive-aggressive condemnation in His simple request for me to pay heed.

Ashamed, I apologized. I looked toward the communion table

at the front of the church. It was the symbol of the greatest demonstration of love that any groom bestowed upon a bride; His sacrifice on the cross and His victory over death. Jesus clearly demonstrated His everlasting, unwavering love for me two thousand years ago. However, He continues to remind me of that love through His Word and His interaction every day. I felt His forgiveness and an invitation to draw into closer fellowship with Him; it was all that was desired from me that day.

God does not hold resentment or bitterness against my inattentiveness, but His heart aches for intimacy with me. He does not need my love to complete Him; He is complete within Himself. However, He longs for all my heart, all my mind, and my undivided devotion as He draws near to me.

## The Storm Chasers

One humid summer evening, my friend and I escaped into the air-conditioned comfort of Walmart. After a leisurely trip up and down every aisle in the store, we reluctantly took our purchases to the longest checkout counter, hesitant to head back out into the sticky heat. As we waited in line, I could see that a rain shower had passed through while we were shopping. The sun shone through the dispelling clouds even though thunder still rumbled in the distance.

As we soon found out upon leaving the store, the brief shower had done little to break the humidity. We placed our groceries in the back of the car and rolled down the windows to catch a breeze. We could see the dark clouds just beyond us. On a whim, my friend suggested we go for a drive. We could follow the storm at a safe distance. As we drove along, we regaled each other with storm stories from our childhoods, and we became more determined to find a good vantage point to watch the distant thunder and lightning. We longed for a good old-fashioned God-created firework display!

After driving miles out of our way, we came to the

disappointing conclusion that we'd never be able to catch the elusive storm clouds. We headed home in bright sunlight. By the time we reached my neighborhood, a few clouds had rolled in once more, but they didn't appear to hold much promise of rain. We made quick work of carrying my groceries up to my suite as my friend was parked in a no-parking zone, and I bid her a hasty good-bye.

As soon as the door shut behind me, a huge wall of wind violently pounded against my balcony window. Huge ink-black clouds hung low in the sky. The lights flickered once or twice, and I found myself in darkness. In less than five minutes, the storm passed. As I gazed across the horizon at the vanishing clouds, I felt a nudge in my spirit. I felt the Lord gently teasing me. "You were chasing something you were never going to find by your own efforts, and now here it is. My roar was right behind you."

When our pursuit of God focuses mainly on demonstrations of His power, we will eventually become discouraged and frustrated. God desires that we seek His face more than we seek His deeds. (1 Kings 19:1-13). If we are chasing a relationship with the God who happens to delight in demonstrating His love for us and those we love in practical, tangible ways, our pursuit will never be in vain.

## A Cup of Water in My Name

Our church held a very unusual service one Sunday. We met outdoors to serve our neighbours. We raised a few tents, prepared a stage for the worship band, and fired up several barbecues. It was our second annual "Carnival of Hope."

We sent out flyers earlier that month, inviting our neighbours to join us for a free garage sale. Face painting, a petting zoo, haircuts for school kids, family photographs, and delicious homemade treats would be available at no charge. A bus with PlayStation games promised to keep teens happy. Several hand-painted signs declared, "Everything is free! Come and eat all you want! Take all you want!" In case the message was missed, we even had business cards available that explicitly stated that there was no charge. We had no motivations beyond a desire to bless our neighbours. All the items laid out for the garage sale were of good quality. There was absolutely no junk, and there were no broken items.

At noon, we officially opened. Hundreds of people filed through the gates throughout the afternoon. Garbage bags quickly filled with clothes; boxes were loaded with toys, books, and small kitchen appliances. Refurbished computers found their way into the arms of school children. Winter coats and boots were briefly tried on in the blazing heat. Hot dogs were devoured; homemade cookies, cakes, and squares were sampled, and the drink station was hopping. Face-painted children held balloon animals as they sat quietly for their back-to-school haircuts.

In the midst of the joyful chaos, I was drawn to an older First-Nations woman dressed in the tradition of the elders of her community. She wore a dark headscarf, a long heavy skirt, and a thick sweater. There wasn't much shade, and she was sweltering. Wearily, she sat on the grass and tried to fill a torn grocery bag with the items she had selected from the garage sale. I handed her a larger bag, then talked with her briefly before realizing her understanding of English was limited. With an apologetic smile, I started back toward my volunteer station.

As I turned to leave the woman, the Lord nudged me. He wanted me to bless her. A garbage bag just wasn't enough. I felt I needed a new excuse to approach her. I didn't want her to feel that she had a crazy white woman invading her space while she tried to cope with the heat. Water! That's what she needed! I sped across the grassy field in my power chair and grabbed two bottles of cold water and returned to her side.

I wanted to make eye contact; I wanted to make heart contact, but all I could do was to offer the water bottles with a smile. Her eyes misted over, and she enthusiastically thanked me for my gift with a nod of her head and a sweet smile in reply. We both knew she wasn't just thanking me for the water.

Through the smile of an elderly woman, God smiled His thanks my way.

## *Don't Sweat the Small Stuff*

One day, a friend invited me for coffee. We hadn't seen each other for a while and so she filled me in on her adult children, their lives, and their news. She admitted that she was experiencing 'Empty Nest Syndrome', and while she appreciated the time she could now spend focusing on her husband, she missed her children terribly.

She missed the seemingly mundane conversations around the supper table. She missed those little teachable moments as she taught her children how to cook, how to do laundry, and other household chores. She yearned for those quiet days of just hanging out with her kids in the back yard. Although she knew their emerging independence and self-sufficiency were healthy and natural, she also knew she had decades of life experience that her children could probably tap into as they began families of their own. If only they'd ask.

Just as we were finishing our chat, she casually spoke this little nugget of truth. She said, "I think I understand how God must feel. His children think they have outgrown the need to chat with Him about all their daily joys, worries, and ordinary decisions. Perhaps they don't want to bother Him with trivial matters. I wonder if God's Father-heart aches at times. I wonder if He misses His kids coming to Him with the small stuff."

A child is truly blessed if they have a wise earthly father to whom they can call upon for occasional wisdom and guidance. However, as they mature, they learn to call upon him for such advice less and less. They must learn to make their own way in the world. In contrast, as Christians move toward spiritual maturity, they become more dependent on God's guidance. A mature believer leans heavily upon God's wisdom and direction in their everyday dealings and takes the time to seek His counsel.

John Wesley stated it best. *"When I was young I was sure of everything; in a few years, having been mistaken a thousand times, I was not half so sure of most things as I was before; at present, I am hardly sure of anything but what God has revealed to me."*

## THE FIELD GOD GIVES

There is something magical about a fresh blanket of snow in a large urban centre. The dirty, grimy snow piles on the side of the road are camouflaged for a day or so, until the soot from traffic sullies the new snowfall. Formerly barren, brown, and grey school fields sparkle in the bright winter sunlight.

I remember staring out a classroom window one afternoon when I was a child. A thick blanket of fluffy white snow had fallen on my schoolyard while the class was in session. It was hard for me to concentrate on math that day. I silently begged recess to come quickly, and I kept one eye on the clock. Most of my classmates were just as distracted as I was. When the bell rang, we pulled on sweaters, mitts, scarves, boots, and coats, buttoning and zipping our jackets as we ran out the door and down the stairs. Fresh snow!

Several of my classmates ran straight ahead, but I held back for the briefest of moments. I was overwhelmed by all the possibilities for fun that lay before me, and yet I was reluctant to sully the blanket of snow by trampling on it. The sound of my name being called from further down the field helped me overcome my hesitation, and I joined a group of girls making a line of snow angels. Too soon, recess was over, and we trudged back to our classroom. With a sigh, I slipped into my desk as I glanced out the window at the now quiet schoolyard. Hundreds of little feet and hands had made good use of the snow, and nothing more than our muddy footprints remained.

Snowfall, no matter how beautiful, only offers temporary camouflage for what lies below the pristine surface. When the spring thaw comes, the ugly grime and pollution that the city endured during the winter months lays exposed for all to see. Spring snow quickly melts into the soot, creating murky puddles that lay in wait for an inattentive pedestrian who walks beside any roadway.

Praise God! His forgiveness does not just hide our sins, leaving our filthy stains just under the surface, ready to be exposed by the heat of condemnation. God's cleansing forgiveness and grace seep into the core of our being, bringing purity and freshness from the inside out. The moment we come to Him in repentance, we are made 'pure and white, clean and bright.' He makes all things new. (Revelation 21:5.)

## *A Thousand May Fall at Your Side*

Psalm 91:1 - *"He who dwells in the shelter of the Most High will abide in the shadow of the Almighty. I will say to the LORD, "My refuge and my fortress, my God, in whom I trust."*

When we approach life from the position of remaining under God's sheltering wings, we have the assurance that God carries us through even life's most difficult challenges. When our faith rests on God's faithfulness, we cannot be shaken.

When our faith depends on the behaviour of those around us, God will allow our faith to be shaken. He allows no idols, no matter how innocent those heroes may appear. If your faith is built on the teachings of a favourite theologian, if your picture of God's character is based solely on the example of a beloved pastor, if you can only be drawn into worship through a particular style of music, you will be shaken.

Unfortunately, I am well acquainted with the pain and struggle one feels upon learning their pastor fell into sin. I have been victimized by believers who chose to sacrifice their integrity to the god of prestige. When rumours surfaced that a friend who happened to be a prominent Christian recording artist had an affair, I stoutly defended him. When he finally confessed his sin, I was deeply disappointed but I continued to pray as he was slowly restored to ministry over several years. A beloved Christian writer who authored several self-help books for those who struggled to deepen their relationship with God was exposed as an abuser. He admitted that he sexually abused several of his counselling clients.

God remained faithful, and His character did not change in the midst of these betrayals. Somehow I clung to His truth, and He carried me through. And yet, I have witnessed the fall of many believers as their Christian heroes fell before them. Why did I remain relatively unshaken? I don't honestly know. My response to these betrayals of trust was not always perfect. God never failed me. Perhaps I was resting under His wings more than I knew. One thing I do know, the more I place my trust in God, the less I am shaken by the sinful actions of Christian leaders and mentors. As I build my house on the firm foundation of God's Word, I can withstand all storms that threaten to destroy my trust in God and man.

1 Timothy 3:12-17 - *"Indeed, all who desire to live a godly life in Christ Jesus will be persecuted, while evil people and impostors will go on from bad to worse, deceiving and being deceived. But as for you,*

*continue in what you have learned and have firmly believed, knowing from whom you learned it and how from childhood you have been acquainted with the sacred writings, which are able to make you wise for salvation through faith in Christ Jesus. All Scripture is breathed out by God and profitable for teaching, for reproof, for correction, and for training in righteousness, that the man of God may be complete, equipped for every good work."*

## The Farmer's Gamble

Although my parents left farming life and moved into the city before I was born, I grew up surrounded by their farmer friends. Some of my fondest childhood memories were weekend trips to the farm of a couple that I considered my aunt and uncle although we were not related by blood. I continued using the term of endearment into my adulthood.

As I listened to the adults talk on the front porch of the old farmhouse, I became aware of the ebb and flow of the seasons. Early spring snowfalls would slowly melt into the thawing ground, providing rich nutrients that farmers affectionately called 'a poor man's fertilizer.' Although the moisture would postpone planting in the short growing season, this late snow was always welcome in the semi-arid southern Alberta region. The cool northern spring would turn into a blazing hot summer, which brought the risk of drought, hail, and pestilence.

When autumn approached and the nights grew colder, I sensed tension build. It was time for the farmer's annual gamble. When should they harvest? Too long of a delay ran the risk of early snows weighing down the crops, resulting in a small yield.

Harvesting too soon meant the crops might not fully ripen, which would also lead to lower yield. My farming friends were at the mercy of the fickle Alberta weather. Decades later, their sons and daughters faced the same uncertainty despite technological advances. It was anyone's guess, and they could only rely on experience.

Unlike my farming friends, Christians have an unfailing promise. If we strengthen our hearts and resolve not to yield to the temptation of harvesting before crops are ripe, the Lord will accomplish His work in our lives and the lives of those around us.

Isaiah 55:10-11 - *"For as the rain and the snow come down from heaven and do not return there but water the earth, making it bring forth and sprout, giving seed to the sower and bread to the eater, so shall my word be that goes out from my mouth; it shall not return to me empty, but it shall accomplish that which I purpose, and shall succeed in the thing for which I sent it."*

God has given us His blessing. He has put His stamp of approval on our hearts, and we can rest assured He will never withdraw His promises from us.

2 Corinthians 1: 18-22 - *"As surely as God is faithful, our word to*

*you has not been Yes and No. For the Son of God, Jesus Christ, whom we proclaimed among you, Silvanus and Timothy and I, was not Yes and No, but in him it is always Yes. For all the promises of God find their Yes in him. That is why it is through him that we utter our Amen to God for His glory. And it is God who establishes us with you in Christ, and has anointed us, and who has also put His seal on us and given us His Spirit in our hearts as a guarantee."*

You can take that promise to the bank!

## Maintain Your Blessing

James 1:17 – *"Every good gift and every perfect gift is from above, coming down from the Father of lights with whom there is no variation or shadow due to change."*

Imagine that a father bestows the same gift on his two beloved children. Each son is given a brand-new sturdily built house, fully furnished and in top condition. The homes, if properly maintained, can withstand gale-force winds, driving rain and blizzards that periodically frequent the area. Each son is given the necessary finances, tools, training, and manuals needed to maintain their homes for a lifetime. The father provides a network of contractors and artisans available for consultation when problems arise. He assures them that they can contact him for advice at any time. His only wish is that they take care of their homes so they can shelter his children and grandchildren. He hoped these homes would be places of hospitality for their friends and family for generations to come.

If you drove past these two homes during the first five or six years, you would see that both sons complied with their father's desire. As the years pass, one son becomes a little lax. After all, his job requires long hours spent away from home, and the weather has been excellent; the winters have been mild and the summers pleasant. The old caulking around the windowpanes begins to crack, and the eavestroughs sag, not allowing rain water to drain properly. He'd rather spend his fall season watching football than climbing a ladder to clear away leaves and debris from the eave's troughs. A few tiny seedlings from flowering trees nearby have sprouted up close to the foundation of the home. The homeowner barely has time to give his yard a glance due to time constraints of his new job.

In contrast, his younger brother finds a new job closer to home, cutting back on his commute. Although maintaining a home requires a steep learning curve, he learns to trust the advice of his father. After a few years of spending two or three hours a week caring for his home, he knows every nook and cranny of his abode and is quick to spot any potential trouble areas.

A few more years pass. The main-floor windows of the older brother's home are hard to see from the street as the seedlings have grown into small trees, their roots digging deep alongside the foundation walls. Once healthy young trees died from a lack of water and fertilizer. The roof shingles look tattered and worn, and the eavestrough now has open gaps. There has been some trouble with the drains in the basement, and the home energy bills have skyrocketed. Windows and doors aren't as airtight as they used to be, lessening their efficiency in keeping the elements at bay. The weather-stripping has become hard and brittle.

The younger brother's home still looks much the same as it always did, although the original saplings now soar over the house, providing shade on hot summer days. The trees' root systems are far enough away to not interfere with the foundation. His front porch is a gathering place for his neighbours; they've become good friends over the years. It's easy to get to know your neighbours when you are outside taking care of your yard. A few of them worked together a couple of year's prior, replacing insulation in their attics with a better quality product.

That year, severe weather hits their town. Winter blizzards batter the houses. Snow, sleet, and hail pound against the windows and rattle the doors. Heavy snow blankets the roofs, and snowdrifts pile high in the yards. During the spring thaw, the snowdrifts slowly melt as water runs off the roofs. It becomes evident that the two brothers' homes have not fared the same.

The exterior of the younger brother's home suffers superficial damage. With the help of family and neighbours, the few shingles that blew away are replaced, a cracked window is reglazed, and the paint is spruced up. A few broken tree limbs are cleared away. The house is as solid as the day it was built, and the basement still provides a dry and cozy refuge for the teenagers in the neighbourhood to congregate. He had no need to dip into the contingency fund his father set up for him years ago. He is able to come to the aid of a couple of his neighbours who suffered more damage than himself by using some of the funds that had been set aside.

Unfortunately, the older brother's house did not fare as well. Extensive damage from ice dams caused by the poor condition of the roof and eavestroughs has caused water to seep into the attic. Dangerous black mould spores have begun to grow in the remaining sodden insulation. The drains in the basement have overflowed, and when an expert is called in, he discovers that the sewer lines need to be replaced. Tree roots have broken through and plugged the lines. The basement smells musty and unpleasant, and the only time anyone goes down there is to do the laundry. All the windows along the northwest side of the house need to be replaced as the windowsills have rotted away from dampness. The flooring near the front entrance is warped, and the concrete slabs leading to the front door have shifted and cracked. The house isn't very inviting, and the family moves out until repairs can be done. Over the years, the older brother dipped into his contingency fund for a new car and a fancy boat, and he now needs to apply for a mortgage on his home to pay for the repairs.

And so it is in our Christian walk. We are given incredible blessings when we become a member of God's family. (Ephesians 1:3-14) We are given every good gift, and we are provided with every provision we will need to strengthen ourselves. We are given access to all the knowledge we will need to learn se we can live blessed lifes. We are given the heavenly resources that will cause us to prosper.

All He asks is that we remain good stewards of our spiritual home. He asks us that we perform daily maintenance on our dwelling place through the reading of his instruction manual – His Word - and through prayer, service and sacrifice. He asks us to seek out the wisdom of those who have gone before us and to make provision so we can draw from it in time of need.

We easily slip into complacency in the years of abundance. We take for granted the gifts that God has given us. A little slip here, a lack of attention to detail there, combines with a healthy dose of procrastination. Before we know it, we find ourselves in the same predicament as the older brother in our little parable.

Fortunately for us, we don't have to live in a house in disrepair. God can make all things new as we come to Him in humility and repentance. It might take some perseverance on our part, but our Father God will patiently work beside us as we clean up our mess.

## *GIVE, NO MATTER WHAT THE SEASON!*

As political, economic and natural storms cross our planet, Christians band together against the winds that rattle at our doors and howl at our windows. During times of adversity and hardship, when the grey, thick clouds of political strife and international crises loom over us, it is tempting to draw the curtains closed and barricade ourselves from the ugliness outside our doors. When we face severe economic hardship, it can be hard to believe that we have anything of value that we can offer to God and our world.

In times of adversity, God invites His people to work alongside Him. As we venture out, He pours His grace into us, allowing us to be effective agents of His provision. As Christians perform gracious acts of compassion and generosity, God takes these sacrificial gifts and multiplies them for the benefit of the surrounding community. Jesus found much pleasure in the poor widow's offering of a few pennies for the upkeep of the temple, and He is just as blessed by our sacrificial giving during times of hardship.

No matter what storms your community faces today, present

your heart to the Lord, and you'll feel the warmth of His light shine on you and through you. That light will be a beacon to those in the darkness and you'll be given the awesome opportunity to be a messenger of God's love, grace, and compassion to your neighbours!

## Have You Checked Your Insurance Policy?

My rental lease agreement states that I must carry adequate insurance coverage. Every year, I receive a phone call from my insurance agent whose job it is to make sure my policy does indeed provide proper coverage. One year, my agent strongly suggested that I upgrade my policy from the standard coverage to a more comprehensive package. She could sense my reluctance to do so and offered to send me clear documentation that would explain the policy I currently owned and the policy that she felt would better serve my needs.

The informational package provided me with an afternoon's entertainment when it arrived a couple of days later. I was glad to know I was covered against bear vandalism although I wondered how the bear would enter into my suite. Would it take the stairs or the elevator? I was amused to find that my rugs would not be insured against leaking oil damage caused by repairing motor vehicles. I chuckled. "Oh well, there goes my oil-change-from-home business."

While I understand that maintaining adequate coverage is the responsible thing to do, I know the insurance industry capitalizes on the fear of the unknown. What if I die tomorrow? How will my children go to college? Will I have a roof over my head if a flood ravages my town? What if I am in a horrible accident, and I am crippled for the rest of my life? What if I am behind the wheel in a car crash? What if my apartment is burglarized, and I lose all my possessions? What if confused and directionally challenged bears attack my high-rise in the middle of a large, urban city?

Christians have assurance for today and not just insurance against the 'what-ifs' of tomorrow. We can safely place our hopes and fears in His capable hands. As we submit our ways to the Lord and follow through on His guidance and direction, we avert self-caused tragedy. Although we might face calamity and natural disasters at some point in our future, we can be assured - His promises will see us through.

Jeremiah 29:11 - " *For I know the plans I have for you, declares the Lord, plans for welfare and not for evil, to give you a future and a hope*"

Isaiah 43 1-2 - "*Fear not, for I have redeemed you; I have called you by name, you are mine. When you pass through the waters, I will be with you; and through the rivers, they shall not overwhelm you; when you walk through fire you shall not be burned.*"

Matt 6:31-34 - *"Therefore do not be anxious, saying, 'What shall we eat?' or 'What shall we drink?' or 'What shall we wear?' For the Gentiles seek after all these things, and your heavenly Father knows that you need them all. But seek first the kingdom of God and his righteousness, and all these things will be added to you. Therefore do not be anxious about tomorrow, for tomorrow will be anxious for itself. Sufficient for the day is its own trouble."*

## The Long and Winding Road

I accompanied a friend as she traveled to her mother's interment in a cemetery that is about a two-hour drive away from our city. Relatives who lived close by invited us to join them for a quick cup of coffee after the service. Our host assured us that he would lead us to his new home, and we agreed to follow him. Within two minutes, he was so far ahead of us that we could barely see his truck.

After twenty minutes, I began to think that this side trip was not such a good idea. My friend was exhausted. The road wound its way around hilly farmland, and we could only catch a glimpse of our guide each time he slowed down to indicate we were changing directions. We soon realized that without his guidance, we would be lost. As the sky was thick with clouds, we could not gauge the direction we were headed, and each turn confused us more. We knew we had a two-hour trip ahead of us once we backtracked our way to the main road after our stop for the promised quick cup of coffee. At that point, we doubted we could find our way back to the freeway.

Gradually, farmland gave way to industrial parks, and we

realized our guide had led us well. Our host lived in a small town just off the highway. By taking the back roads, we avoided rush hour traffic, we had time to visit with my friend's family, and we would still be on our way long before nightfall.

God often reminds me that He is my faithful guide. When the road becomes confusing, I cannot rely on my sense of spiritual direction. When anxiety rises, and the enemy whispers in my ear that it'd be wiser for me to do my own navigating, God asks me to trust His guidance. When I can't see beyond the bend in the road, God asks me to surrender my roadmap to Him. God has never led me astray.

Proverbs 16:9 - *"The heart of man plans his way, but the Lord establishes his steps."*

Proverbs 3:5-6 - *"Trust in the Lord with all your heart and lean not on your own understanding; In all your ways acknowledge Him, and He will make your paths straight. in all your ways acknowledge him, and he will make your paths straight."*

## *Our God Longs For Us*

Some believe the God of the Old Testament is distant, cold, and judgmental. They prefer the God of the New Testament - the wooing, tender-hearted God who stands with His arms wide open to welcome anyone and everybody home, no questions asked. In my childhood, I carried the same view of God as I listened to epic Bible stories of Adam and Eve, Noah, and the great Exodus. Even after I entered into a deeper relationship with God, I found it difficult to reconcile the God of the Old Testament with the New Testament God Who sent His Son to die in our place.

I am sure that if I had sat down and thought about it, I would have realized the core premise of my thesis was flawed. After all, I knew God was unchanging, and He was perfect in all His ways. If this was true, logic dictates that He did not undergo a massive character makeover between the last verse of Malachi and the first verse of Matthew. His passionate desire to reconcile with His people was as strong on the day He banished Adam and Eve as it was on the day He watched His Son agonizing in the garden of Gethsemane. *"For I am the Lord, I change not"* Malachi 3:6.

God dismantled my beliefs by leading me through the books of Genesis, Exodus, and Deuteronomy for one week. I set aside my study Bible and picked up a modern language version in its stead. I read the books in the same way I would read any other story. Whenever I began to read through the lens of past Bible studies, I felt a nudge. "Read on, I have more to show you, reserve your judgment until you read the rest of the story!" The familiar accounts of Adam and Eve, Cain and Abel, Enoch, Noah, Abraham and Sarah, Isaac, Esau, Rebecca, Joseph and his brothers, and the squabbling children of Israel in the desert all took on new meaning.

I had to set the Bible down to compose myself as I read. I was overwhelmed by God's all-consuming desire to be in a relationship with His creation. It broke my heart as I saw those He loved most betray Him. God kept on loving.

Deuteronomy 7:7 - *"It was not because you were more in number than any other people that the Lord set his love on you and chose you, for you were the fewest of all peoples, but it is because the Lord loves you and is keeping the oath that he swore to your fathers, that the Lord has brought you out with a mighty hand and redeemed you from the house of slavery, from the hand of Pharaoh king of Egypt."*

He kept on hoping, and He kept on forgiving.

Exodus 34:6-7a - *"The Lord, the Lord, a God merciful and gracious, slow to anger, and abounding in steadfast love and faithfulness, keeping steadfast love for thousands, forgiving iniquity and transgression and sin."*

I was astounded at the blatant sin and rebellion of His creation. I was stunned by the haughty disdain that met His gracious overtures of reconciliation. He passionately longed for His people. His holy jealousy demanded that their hearts be as fully committed to His heart as His heart was committed to theirs. The God of the Old Testament was not cold and distant at all! He was present, passionate, and relentless in His pursuit of their affection. His one desire was to restore His creation back to Himself.

His heart broke as His children turned their hearts away from Him. He grieved as they allowed themselves to be enticed away into unfulfilling servitude to false gods. Those gods demanded complete allegiance and gave nothing in return.

People say that they admire Jesus, but they don't like the God of the Old Testament that much. However, Jesus thought highly of our Heavenly Father and spoke of Him with great affection and trust. Jesus went as far to say on several occasions that He only did what the Father had shown him. All the loving, tender, forgiving, and life-transforming acts Jesus performed on this earth were by request of the God of the Old Testament. Every word that Jesus spoke against prejudice and oppression was dictated to Him by the God of the Old Testament.

This same God longs to come to you as Immanuel, God with us. He paid the ransom for your sin and debt. Your desire to be in a relationship with Him is only a tiny ember compared to His burning desire to be in intimate, passionate, holy communion with you.

## *He Knows the Rest of Our Story*

I commiserated with a friend as we discussed current events in our lives. We are members of the same church, and we both share a deep sense of gratitude for the inspiring teaching we receive every week. A few months earlier, our pastor challenged our church to deepen our commitment to see Christ's love demonstrated in our neighbourhoods and communities. We both accepted the challenge, and we were wise enough to know that God would take us at our word.

Within a week of renewing my commitment to be a light in my neighbourhood, I experienced a disconcerting encounter with a new neighbour in my apartment building. I came away feeling shaken and vulnerable. I struggled to walk past my fears so I could follow the Lord's marching orders. My friend's experience was more harrowing than mine, and she too confessed to feeling inadequate for the task ahead of us.

We agreed that the business of being a light-bearer was a messy, uncertain, and confusing one. We heard testimonies of miraculous results in the neighbourhoods of other congregants who stood with us that Sunday morning. Neither one of us could stand up in front of our church with our testimonies.

We both knew we were still in the midst of our stories. We couldn't gauge our success by our circumstances. We knew the dangers of comparing our stories with the stories being played out in the lives of our brothers and sisters in Christ. We put our trust in the One who called us forward, and we kept our eyes fixed on Him. Because He is the Author of our lives, His plans and purposes will come to fruition. (Hebrews 12:2, Isaiah 55:11) He has the advantage of seeing our stories from the beginning to the end. He sees beyond the mire and chaos of the middle of our stories, and He has the power to see us through to the completion of His word.

Are you struggling to remain obedient and faithful to God's calling? Have you made a commitment to Him only to find your world turned up-side-down? Are you wondering how you can clear a path so you can sort out the mess? Does the victory seem impossible? Take God at His word.

Jeremiah 29:11-14 - *"For I know the plans I have for you, declares the Lord, plans for welfare and not for evil, to give you a future and a hope. Then you will call upon me and come and pray to me, and I will hear you. You will seek me and find me, when you seek me with all your heart. I will be found by you, declares the Lord, and I will restore your fortunes and gather you from all the nations and all the places where I have driven you and I will bring you back to the place from which I sent you into exile."*

## The Master's Touch

The landscape designer of a condominium building near my apartment deserves an apology from me. Playing armchair gardener, I turned my nose up at one of his bedding selections one year. One plant was low to the ground, with no flowers and huge muddy green leaves in its first spring. The plant remained relatively the same throughout the growing season. As it didn't spread, it didn't serve as a background for the flowering plants that shared its bed. Dull, listless, and limp, even the artistically placed white stones scattered around the plants didn't change my opinion that the droopy plants were duds. That is, until one week in mid-October.

We were well into autumn, and most trees had dropped their colourful foliage due to an early frost. Taking advantage of a relatively mild day, I navigated my way to my local shopping centre to stock up on items I would need for winter. As I approached the condominium's flowerbed, I stopped in my tracks. The once nondescript foliage appeared to have been painted by a creative genius overnight; the dark green leaves served as the perfect canvas, enhancing each masterful brush stroke. Deep purples, browns, and russets popped against the white rocks that lined the bed. Now, the landscaper's plan made sense to me, and I breathed a word of apology under my breath to the unseen genius.

I find it laughable that some people think Christianity as a strict and rigid religion. I find it absurd that my God would be considered as inflexible, disinterested and stoic. A non-believer might be forgiven for such a misbelief. Their eyes have not yet been opened to the truth.

Examples of God's creativity leap from His Word. From the first chapter of Genesis to the very last verse of Revelation, we are shown a God who is always creating. He specializes in transforming the mundane into the sublime. From dust, He formed man; from water He made wine. He took our diseased and hardened hearts and made us into new creations. From death, He brought life. With a God like this, why would we ever expect our lives to be predictable and dull? Even through seasons that appear colourless and gray, God breathes new life.

## *Come See What You Gave Me!*

I find great pleasure in gift giving. I love to search the Internet and scour catalogues, looking for meaningful gifts for my friends and family. I take the Lord shopping with me, chatting away in prayer with Him, asking Him to guide me to the perfect gift for each person on my list. I consider it a joy to be able to give to someone else. It's just the way God made me.

As much as I love to shop for others, I like to watch people open those gifts even more. As a young teen, I'd lay awake on Christmas Eve in gleeful anticipation. I could hardly wait to see the expressions of each family member as they opened my present to them. I now have the occasional joy of watching my young nephews and nieces open gifts on Christmas Day. A hasty but heartfelt, "Wow! Thanks, Auntie!" yelled across the room by a preschooler as he rips into a building set is all I need to hear.

My heart melts when the recipient of the gift invites me to join in the fun. One Christmas afternoon, long after the gifts had been opened, and the wrapping paper was discarded, I felt the tug of a tiny hand on my sweater sleeve. My four-year-old nephew implored, "Auntie Kath, come and see, come and see what you gave to me!" He led me into his little sanctuary that was tucked away in a corner of my sister's den. There, he had set up the beginner building set I had given him that morning.

I sat in a nearby chair to marvel at his work, but that was not good enough for him. Tugging at my arm again, he insisted I sit on the floor with him, and so I did. I was a willing and besotted captive audience to his childish prattle. He carefully explained just how everything worked and then invited me to show him how to build a tower. He had no idea the gift he was giving me at that moment was much larger than any material possession I had given him. Later on, his two-year-old sister snuggled in my arms as she cuddled the stuffed bear I had given her. Together, we looked at the storybook that had come with the bear, comparing the book's illustrations with the bear in her arms. My auntie's heart was full to the brim and running over.

God lavishes good gifts on me, just because I am His child. Many of His gifts are given so I can use them to bless others. The gift of mercy, hospitality, evangelism, a generous spirit, healing, and the list goes on. He blessed me with creativity, and He gave me an appreciation of created beauty. Many of His gifts are intended for me to employ in my personal life: the gifts of salvation, forgiveness, redemption, sanctification, and transformation. The most precious of all the gifts He has lavished upon me is the gift of His unfettered, unconditional love.

My Heavenly Father is pleased when I thank Him for the gifts He has bestowed upon me. I believe His heart rejoices even more when I invite Him to join me in my private sanctuary as I learn to use the gifts He has given.

## Serving in Assured Authority

Junior High School is brutal. Peer pressure is intense, hormones rage, and classrooms can easily erupt into battlefields. Your attire, speech, appearance, and social status are under constant scrutiny. Instant judgments are made, and labels are hard to shake. There is little mercy in this brutal arena.

Yes, the task of being the teacher of junior high school students is best left to the brave at heart and those of a stout constitution.

I remember the day I came to this astute observation. On the first day of school, three pubescent boys decided to test the power of their newfound height by attempting to intimidate our diminutive math teacher, who was approaching retirement. Barely batting an eyelash, Miss Thompson flung a sharpened pencil with lightning speed in the direction of the ringleader. It whizzed by his ear within millimetres and struck its intended target - the bulletin board right behind the troublemaker's head. Maintaining eye contact with the boy, Miss Thompson indicated he should take his seat and with a warm smile, asked him to open up his book to chapter one. Her praise was just as quick as her discipline, and we thrived under her tutelage. Miss

Thompson suffered no fools, but she was one of the most beloved teachers in our school. We felt respected and loved, and she had an open door policy after class for those of us who struggled with math.

Upon her retirement at the end of the next school year, the same three lads were part of the committee that purchased our school's going away gift. Although Miss Thompson was now a good foot shorter than any of those boys, they gladly submitted to her quiet authority when she asked them to return to their seats at the conclusion of their presentation.

Miss Thompson never resorted to manipulation, guilt trips, insults, screaming or idle threats to assert her authority. Not only had she gained the respect of her students, she earned the trust of our principal. He knew that she would make sure that her students fully understood his directives. She knew the task that had been given to her and was faithful to carry it out.

Jesus spoke out of an assuredness of His authority, for He only spoke and did as His Father instructed. *"I tell you the truth, the Son can do nothing by himself; he can do only what he sees his Father doing, because whatever the Father does the Son also does."* John 5:19. His authority was recognized by others, not only because of His insightful teaching but because He successfully confronted sickness, demon-possession, injustice and sin - the bullies of His day. Jesus wielded His authority through acts of quiet service. Jesus had no need to resort to shoddy tactics and crowd manipulation. He spoke the hard truth with the loving intention of bringing freedom and healing to those that heard.

God has entrusted the same authority to us that He gave Jesus but only insofar we submit our lives to Him. Jesus' authority was born out of intimacy with His Father and His willingness to carry out His Father's directives.

Perhaps, you are struggling in your role as a leader. May you draw close to the Father and allow Him to mentor you through His Word. As you allow Him to lead you into His heart for you, you will be able to lead others into the same place of quiet assuredness and peace.

## *So, What Do You Do?*

In my parent's time, it was common for strangers to exchange the formal greeting of "How do you do?" Although this salutation might be used elsewhere in the English-speaking world, it is seldom used in North America today. The more informal, "It's nice to meet you," has taken its place in most social settings. As the small talk of first introductions continues, the next question commonly asked is "So, what do you do?"

A guest presenter or writer is introduced to their audience by a brief description of what the speaker does for a living and a short synopsis of their personal life.

"Please welcome John, the father of three, who has been married to his lovely wife, Jane, for thirteen years. John is a respected business owner."

"Please welcome Julie. Julie studied at Harvard and is an avid gardener. Her most recent Ph.D. makes her a welcome addition to our panel today."

"Please welcome Katherine, we aren't quite sure what she does, but perhaps you can glean something from what she's about to share."

I have not held a traditional job for over thirty years. I can't list my professional accomplishments, and I don't have degrees behind my name. I am not married, and I can't extol the virtues of my nonexistent husband. I have no children, so I don't carry family photos of my kids. I have limited contact with my extended family as they live far from me.

Although I consider my Internet work to be a full-time ministry, I have no staff to boast of, and it is difficult for me to assess my impact. Unlike an evangelist at a crusade, it is impossible for me to estimate the lives that I've reached for the kingdom. I don't know how many prayers have been answered through my ministry. Sometimes, I feel what I have to offer the world is insignificant in comparison to Bible scholars, speakers, and writers who have touched my life.

However, God challenges me to walk past my insecurities and my feelings of inadequacy. He can multiply my small offering of five loaves and two fishes to feed those who are hungry for His word. A mighty giant was toppled by an obscure shepherd who honed his skill as an adept marksman while working in hidden fields. God used a little boy's lunch; God used one small stone, and God uses me.

I Corinthians 1:27-29 - *"God chose what is foolish in the world to shame the wise; God chose what is weak in the world to shame the strong; God chose what is low and despised in the world, even things that are not, to bring to nothing things that are, so that no human being might boast in the presence of God."*

## CULTIVATING KINDNESS

Gaining knowledge is a messy business for children. A toddler must drop food, toys, soothers and cups from their high chair dozens of times before they are satisfied that the Law of Gravity holds true in all circumstances. What goes down stays down unless picked up by the toddler's ever patient and obliging lab assistant, such as a parent or an older sibling. A discerning yet thirsty child learns that only pointing in the direction of the fridge will not produce the same result as pointing at the fridge with his Sippy-Cup in his free hand.

Children are in constant search of willing test subjects in their experiments, learning much from their subject's response to stimuli they provide. A child conducts thousands of such tests before he ever enters kindergarten. While some studies involve the exploration of the physical world around him, many of his trials and studies are purely sociological in nature. Through trial and error, he learns how to interact with those who share his world, beginning with his parents, and then his siblings, then his extended family, and finally, those in his community.

In the same manner that a child learns how to ask for a glass of milk, he learns the joys of cultivating the fruit of the Spirit in his heart. A wise parent swiftly provides enthusiastic, positive reinforcement when a child exhibits even the smallest inclination toward developing these skills. A child that is coaxed into walking by warm smiles, eager expressive faces and loving, outstretched arms will usually take his first steps sooner than a child who is left to his own devices. A child who receives encouraging, focused responses to simple acts of kindness is more likely to continue this behaviour in the future.

It may take a mother several hours to clean her kitchen after a Mother's Day breakfast that was lovingly prepared by her children. She may have to choke down burned toast and swallow a few eggshells along with her scrambled eggs. A wise mother gathers her children in her arms for hugs and kisses, then raves over their culinary attempts, ignoring the residue of sticky fingers that clutch her.

Kindness is a skill that must be learned, and it is best learned through reinforcement. As a child matures, he learns that kindness is a reward in itself, and he learns that he should not always expect each act of kindness to receive an enthusiastic and overt response of gratitude.

However, recipients of kindness should be attentive and

receptive with grateful and genuine hearts. If we desire to live in an atmosphere of kindness, then we should nurture this quality. Although it is not always possible to acknowledge every gesture, we can respond to deliberate acts of kindness with more than a mumbled 'thank you' under our breath.

Making eye contact as we thank the person who holds the elevator door for us in the morning rush blesses the door-opener and anyone else in the elevator who was momentarily delayed. A friendly nod and a two-finger wave of thanks to the person who allows us to merge into their traffic lane brings more good will on the roadway than a nasty glare at a driver who failed to let us into traffic. A husband will probably respond more favourably to a quick hug and a soft kiss on the cheek along with a 'thank you' after he puts his dirty mug in the dishwasher instead of a dismissive grunt and a sarcastic remark about all the other chores he failed to do.

I hear people say they long for a kinder, gentler world in which to live. I wonder how much kinder the world around us would be if we resolved to be alert to daily kindnesses we already experience.

## RELISHING OBSCURITY

Colossians 3:3-4 (MSG) – *"Your old life is dead. Your new life, which is your real life—even though invisible to spectators—is with Christ in God. He is your life. When Christ (your real life, remember) shows up again on this earth, you'll show up, too—the real you, the glorious you. Meanwhile, be content with obscurity, like Christ."*

I am content in obscurity. If anything, I crave it. I am happy to be hidden in Christ, stepping forward to do His bidding when called, then retreating until I receive His orders yet again. There is safety in obscurity. I am hidden in His robes of righteousness. I am safe from the harsh spotlight of the devil's scrutiny. No matter how the enemy tries to dig into my past to find the juicy dirt, he cannot find any. My files are closed and sealed.

However, if I were to step ahead of God to bring the focus on myself rather than on the One I serve, I would step past that protection. Unfortunately, I have learned this truth through witnessing brothers and sisters in Christ fall into the fowler's snare. With a broken heart and a grieving spirit, I have watched international leaders of Christian organizations, worship leaders, writers, local pastors, missionaries in far-away villages and Sunday school teachers become deceived. They lost perspective, forgetting that they were only messengers of the One who holds the power to transform and heal, restore and resurrect.

Recognition from other people is sweet, but when we begin to pursue the praise of others, recognition becomes the bait in the enemy's snare. The Bible says we cannot serve two masters. Either we are a bond slave to Jesus, or we are a slave to those from whom we crave recognition and accolades.

Considering the countless scandals covered in today's media, I have come to the following conclusions. If we allow ourselves to be moulded into the image that others make for us, we will eventually lose ourselves. As we constantly reinvent ourselves to fit into their idea of who we should be, we will eventually lose any sense of our original identity and purpose, and we will self-destruct. If we submit ourselves to Christ, we also will lose ourselves, but in return, we will gain so much more as we are transformed into His image.

## GOD IS GOOD, ALWAYS!

Shortly before her death Betsie Ten Boom shared a simple truth with her sister, a revelation that profoundly affected the way Corrie lived her life. She mentioned this truth in several of her books and her speaking engagements.

"Often I have heard people say, *'How good God is! We prayed that it would not rain for our church picnic, and look at the lovely weather!'* Yes, God is good when He sends good weather. But God was also good when He allowed my sister, Betsie, to starve to death before my eyes in a German concentration camp. I remember one occasion when I was very discouraged there. Everything around us was dark, and there was darkness in my heart. I remember telling Betsie that I thought God had forgotten us. 'No, Corrie,' said Betsie, 'He has not forgotten us. Remember His word: 'For as the heavens are high above the earth, so great is His steadfast love toward those who fear Him.' There is an ocean of God's love available – there is plenty for everyone. May God grant you never to doubt that victorious love – whatever the circumstances."

Although I have not faced anything close to the horrors of a Nazi concentration camp, I have faced times of darkness and discouragement. I have been betrayed and rejected by those who I counted as my intimate friends and fellow workers in Christ. I helplessly sat as I watched my best friend, a beautiful mother of two, die of cancer. I watched as her family fell apart after her death. I have witnessed great injustices and prejudices. I have seen loved ones sink further into the ravages of sin despite prayer and fasting for them. I have slipped into the dark seas of depression on more than one occasion. I have not drowned in my despair, and I have not given up and walked away.

Those who know me well say that I am just too stubborn to give up, and I tend to agree with them. However, I also believe in His innate goodness. His goodness is as much a part of His nature as my brown eyes are a part of my physical make-up. Dark and confusing circumstances do not change the fundamental nature of God. His mercies, His goodness, and His love never waver.

Long ago, I determined to choose to believe that God is good - always. His goodness has become my anchor. I cannot rely on my circumstances or allow my ever-changing emotions to be my points of reference. I cannot allow my worldview to be determined by anything except His character — His unchanging, trustworthy character.

## *Trying to Find a Way Through?*

Tears streamed down my cheeks as I sat on the stripped bed in my tiny room. My luggage was packed and ready to be taken to the train station. I had made my good-byes the night before, there was nothing left to do but to leave and in the process, leave behind my dreams, my hopes, and my home. I still clung to a faint hope of being used by God in full-time ministry through writing and the creative arts.

Why did everything fall apart? What happened? Looking back now across the years at that broken girl, I now know the answer that girl was not ready to receive. I had determined to make my dream come true in my own strength, and that was my downfall. I had my heart set on reaching my goal, rather than reaching the heart of Jesus. I put work for Christ above relationship with Christ.

Along the way, I allowed my fears and insecurities to be the decision makers in my life. Instead of trusting God's direction as He led me along a different path toward His goals, I tried to return to my comfort zone. It took me a long time to understand that to obey is better than sacrifice. God still had a way to go to reach my heart.

My creativity was buried and hidden in an office in an industrial park in a large urban center. I worked alone; doing routine accounting, answering occasional phone calls and selling books in hopes of keeping our local ministry office running. All the dreams I had thirteen years earlier were still unfulfilled. Although God blessed my work somewhat during those years, and I touched a few hearts, I knew God wasn't fully endorsing my efforts.

I gave up. No matter how I tried to knock down that brick wall of the dead-end in which I found myself, I couldn't make it happen. I gave God the keys to my heart and stepped back. God finally could move.

Now, several years later, the dreams I had as a young, wide-eyed Christian are fulfilled. I'm reaching thousands of people across the world through my writing. I am loved, respected, and needed by my local church. I make a difference. I learned that a dead-end is only a dead-end if you fail to take the turn. I wouldn't have wasted so much energy trying to find my way if I had only stopped and asked for directions. He always knew where He wanted to lead me. He was just waiting for me to allow Him to take the wheel.

## THE YELLOW BOWL BLESSING

I once led a weekly fellowship group in my home. Although I tried to keep the format of the meetings flexible, they tended to fall into a predictable pattern. We would begin with worship, followed by a quick break so people could grab a snack and a drink. After settling back in our chairs with our treats, we would have an ice-breaker question, and then a short teaching time. I always set aside a good portion of time for prayer for personal prayer needs.

I was and still am a firm believer in the power of corporate prayer, and I made sure to share testimonies of answered prayer each week. I became increasingly frustrated when someone would ask for 'just a little blessing'. Just a little blessing? I wondered if they were the type of person who goes through the buffet at a wedding reception, only to return to their table with a small bread and butter plate that holds a cheese slice, a pickle, a couple of lettuce leaves and a sprig of parsley. You just know that the person is driving through a burger joint on his or her way home!

I have a huge yellow bowl I use for making popcorn. Popcorn

was the staple of this home group, and everyone was well acquainted with the bounty this bowl would hold. One week, we diverted from the popcorn routine, and we were happily munching on homemade cookies that someone had brought as a treat. I asked at prayer time, "Does anyone want prayer for anything? If you don't have any specific prayer needs, we would love to gather around you to pray a blessing over you." After a moment of silence, a woman's response caused me to reach my breaking point. She shrugged. "Oh, I guess I could do with just a little blessing…"

Reaching my limit of patience, I abruptly stomped out of my living room and into my kitchen. I am sure my fellowship members were wondering what on earth I was up to, as I rummaged through my cupboards. They were even more bemused when I came back into the room, carrying the popcorn bowl and the smallest bowl I could find in my kitchen.

"What do you want?", I asked my stunned group of friends. "All of God's blessings?" I lifted the popcorn bowl with a flourish. "Or just a 'little blessing?'" It made such an impact that people started asking for a yellow bowl blessing. As their faith grew, so did the audacity of their prayers. We saw God move mightily in our group. Jobs were found; marriages were healed, health was restored.

Matthew 7:7-11 - *"Ask and it will be given to you; seek and you will find; knock and the door will be opened to you. For everyone who asks receives; the one who seeks finds; and to the one who knocks, the door will be opened. Which of you, if your son asks for bread, will give him a stone? Or if he asks for a fish, will give him a snake? If you, then, though you are evil, know how to give good gifts to your children, how much more will your Father in heaven give good gifts to those who ask him!"*

## I Cannot be at Peace Standing Still

I have a terrible sense of balance; it comes with the package of my disability. Standing still in one spot is nearly impossible for me, and I find myself being pulled back and forth. I lean to the left or the right, but I rarely manage to remain still for more than a few seconds at a time. Most of the time, I find myself stepping backwards. Sitting on a fence is difficult as well. I need to grip my hands tightly on the rail. Even then, I find myself swaying as gravity pulls me forward or backward. I worry about falling off my perch, and I am not able to rest.

There have been times when I've tried to sit on the fence when it comes to my relationship with God. I've felt the pull to go back to my old ways of thinking, and my old sin patterns. I've felt tugs of fear, doubt, and shame as they tried to draw me back.

There are times I don't particularly like the road ahead. It looks too hard, too painful, and too challenging, and so I stand still. At least I think I stand still. I find myself taking a step back into my comfort zone as I try to get my balance. I take another step back, as I attempt to calculate the path of least resistance up ahead. All too soon, I find that I have backed myself against a wall. I can't go back to my former identity; my old man is dead. I find myself attracted to side trails that look less demanding. However, walking sideways doesn't get me further along the path.

Walking forward in obedience and trust is my only solution. No matter how difficult God's path appears to be, I know it's the only path of safety for me. I can't stay still. I have three choices: go forward, step backward, or step sideways. I choose to go forward. How about you?

## No Small Thing

Although my disability is a slowly progressive one, the ravages of the neurological condition have taken their toll on my stamina, strength, and dexterity. I am not always aware how far my disability has progressed until I attempt to do something that I was previously able to do, only to discover I can no longer complete the task.

I have been a member of my church for over twenty years. I have rejoiced over the arrivals of much-loved babies. I have watched children grow into young men and women whose hearts burn to serve God and His people. I have grieved over the loss of beloved members of my congregation as deeply as if they were members of my biological family. I have joined with other intercessors in my church as we have prayed victoriously through battles too many to count.

However, as my disability progresses, it seems my contribution to my church diminishes. I'm no longer able to stack chairs and tidy up our school gym after our services; I can't help those in need by providing meals or by performing other practical acts of kindness. As I can't drive, it is not often that I gather with the other intercessors in my church for weekly prayer. There had been times when I have chosen not to attend events as I felt I had nothing to add beyond my presence, and I didn't want to be in the way.

God asks me to stop comparing my contribution to my local body with the contribution of others in the church. As Paul points out in 1 Corinthians 12, God does not let me off the hook from being a functioning part of the body just because I am not a hand or eye. When I despair that I have nothing of worth to contribute, God promises me that if I go where He sends me, He will not send me with empty hands.

I suspect I am not alone in my feelings of inadequacy. Perhaps you wonder if you have anything of value to offer. Perhaps like me, God is encouraging you to seek Him for opportunities to bless others. A simple word spoken in the right season can break through strongholds. A gentle hug can soothe a hurting heart. A handshake can make an newcomer feel a part of the family.

Mark 12:41-44 - *And he sat down opposite the treasury and watched the people putting money into the offering box. Many rich people put in large sums. And a poor widow came and put in two small copper coins, which make a penny. And he called his disciples to him and said to them, "Truly, I say to you, this poor widow has put in more than all those who are contributing to the offering box. For they all contributed out of their abundance, but she out of her poverty has put in everything she had, all she had to live on."*

## *We Bring Pleasure to God's Heart*

Excited giggles, pattering feet and the hushing sounds of Sunday School teachers trying to quiet their eager charges announced the arrival of the children returning to our church sanctuary on Father's Day. As the children scattered throughout the church in search of their parents, I could see they were all carrying gifts for their fathers.

One father was mightily blessed as he had several children. Each child deposited a colourful pop can holder in his lap. John's smile grew larger with each gift. His older boys passed off their gifts with an air of nonchalance and then joined their friends not too far away. They kept their eyes on their father, waiting for his reaction. As John nodded his discreet thanks to each son, each son responded with a slight nod of his own. The nods said it all; the message was received.

His younger children were not worried about ruining any reputation they had with their peers. They surrounded their father, eager to show him the colourful butterflies and other fanciful creatures they had glued on their gifts. Although a few of the decorations were already falling off, John saw past the imperfections. His youngest boy crawled up onto his lap to make sure he had his daddy's full attention. John celebrated his little boy's creativity with gasps of amazement as the tyke pointed out every decoration he had placed on his masterpiece. His daughter kissed him on the cheek and snuggled under his arm as he took the time to thank his children for their gifts. John basked in the love and respect of his children.

Psalm 127:4-6 (MSG) - *"Don't you see that children are God's best gift? The fruit of the womb his generous legacy? Like a warrior's fistful of arrows are the children of a vigorous youth. Oh, how blessed are you parents, with your quivers full of children!"*

Do I bless God even if my offering is imperfect? Do I make His heart proud when I give him the works of my hands? Do my worship and my desire to rest in His presence cause His countenance to shine brighter? According to scripture, it appears I do bring joy to my Father!

Zephaniah 3:17 - *"The Lord your God is in your midst, a mighty one who will save; he will rejoice over you with gladness."*

Psalm 147:11 - *"The Lord takes pleasure in those who fear him, in those who hope in his steadfast love."*

## GOD'S REMEDY FOR BLUE MONDAYS

In 2005, the third Monday of January was declared annual Blue Monday, supposedly the saddest day of the year. This declaration was based on a research study conducted by a British psychologist. The doctor arrived at his conclusion through a complicated formula that involved several factors. First, he factored in the dark, grey, and gloomy weather that blankets the northern hemisphere in January. The sobering realization of serious debt incurred during the holiday shopping season and the post-Christmas holiday letdown as people return to school and work. The failure to keep New Year's resolutions adds to the general feeling of inertia and lack of motivation, according to his study.

Perhaps it is the combination of a strongly determined Celtic heritage on one side of my family tree and a fiercely independent American pioneer background on the other, but I tend to thumb my nose at such studies. Especially when British travel agencies fund those studies in the hopes of selling tropical island vacation packages.

I believe that contentment has little to do with external

circumstances, such as finances or the weather. I praise God that He provided me with a fail-proof remedy for spiritual malaise and the doldrums. He offers this amazing cure to all believers with an ironclad guarantee. If we follow His prescription, we will see positive results.

Encourage yourself in the Lord and be grateful in all circumstances.

1 Thessalonians 5:16-18 - *"Rejoice always, pray without ceasing, give thanks in all circumstances; for this is the will of God in Christ Jesus for you. Do not quench the Spirit."*

Betsie Ten Boom, the beloved sister of Corrie Ten Boom, learned this principle, and then let Corrie in on her secret. I would encourage you to read Corrie's full account of this story in her autobiography, The Hiding Place. In a dark, flea-infested barrack, surrounded by prostitutes, hardened criminals and openly hostile hearts, the Ten Boom sisters put 1 Thessalonians 5:16-18 to the test. Betsie encouraged her stubborn sister to give thanks in all things, even the flea-infested conditions. As these sorely tried saints gave thanks every night, God began to transform the hearts of those around them. Many came to the Lord, and they were able to share the gospel openly from the Bible they kept hidden away from the guards.

Betsie was thankful for the freedom from scrutiny by the guards yet she was puzzled why it was so. One day, she had her answer, and she eagerly shared the good news with her sister.

*"You know, we've never understood why we had so much freedom in the big room,' Betsie said. 'Well, I've found out.' That afternoon, she said, there'd been confusion in her knitting group about sock sizes and they'd asked the supervisor to come and settle it.'But she wouldn't. She wouldn't step through the door and neither would the guards. And you know why?' Betsie could not keep the triumph from her voice: 'Because of the fleas! That's what she said, "That place is crawling with fleas!'*

*My mind rushed back to our first hour in this place. I remembered Betsie's bowed head, remembered her thanks to God for creatures I could see no use for."*

    Boom, Corrie Ten, John L. Sherrill, and Elizabeth Sherrill. *The Hiding Place*. Washington Depot, CT: Chosen, 1971. Print.

## *NO MATTER HOW HARD I TRY...*

I must admit that I am one of the legions of women who tidy up the night before the cleaner is due. I find some solace that a high percentage of people who hire a housecleaner are guilty of the same illogical behaviour. Nevertheless, every month, I scurry around my apartment, dusting and wiping down counters and sinks. Heavens! It would never 'do' for the person whom I pay to clean my apartment to see it in disarray.

No matter how long or how hard I scrub my countertops, I am unable to clean them thoroughly, due to my disability. Faint reminders of coffee and juice stains speckle my counters despite my best efforts. An artfully placed appliance over such a stain might temporarily cover it, but I am well aware of what lies underneath. The corners of the tiled shower collect grime that is simply beyond my physical power to remove. Dust remains on shelves that I cannot reach safely, even though I attempt to clean them with a jury-rigged dust cloth attached to the end of a broom handle. By the time my housecleaner arrives, I am exhausted. Exhaustion soon turns to wry frustration at my foolishness as I watch the stained counter become sparkling clean with a few firm swipes of her cleaning rag. The bathroom grout returns to pristine white by a brief scrubbing.

I also am unable to erase the stain of sin in my life. No amount of good intentions and resolutions will remove them. I cannot hide my guilt under a camouflage of good works. There are dark corners of my heart that provide perfect hiding spots for sin and try as I might, I cannot see them, no matter remove them.

"Our Saviour kneels down and gazes upon the darkest acts of our lives. But rather than recoil in horror, He reaches out in kindness and says, 'I can clean that if you want.' And from the basin of His grace, He scoops a palm full of mercy and washes our sin." Lucado, Max. James - Life Lessons. N.p.: Thomas Nelson, 2007. Print

I think I'll take my Saviour up on His invitation. What about you? Are there sinful areas in your life that are stained and filthy? Are there doors of your heart that you prefer to keep shut because you know of the mess that hides behind those doors? Will you allow the Lord to pour His forgiveness, grace and healing into the very areas that have caused you such guilt and shame?

## Just Do It

1 Corinthians 1:25 - *"For the foolishness of God is wiser than men, and the weakness of God is stronger than men."*

Have you ever realized that you have missed a blessing from God by your inattentiveness to His direction? I have!

It all began with a whisper of a whim of an idea that crossed my mind one morning. "I should apply for a passport." I laughed off the notion as I had no need for such a document. My traveling days as a missionary were long behind me. However, later that day, I found myself visiting the Canadian passport website and I filled out half the application before I abandoned the notion. I was not willing to pay the application fee for a document I would probably never use.

A couple of months later, I joined with believers around the world to pray for a major gathering taking place in Chicago. I would have loved to attend the conference, but I dismissed the idea due to the lack of finances and transportation. I toyed with the idea of registering, but I didn't follow through.

My reluctance to pursue these two inner nudges came back to haunt me. I was given the opportunity to attend the event at the last minute. If I could be ready to leave in less than 36 hours, my transportation and fees would be covered. Unfortunately, even if I had chosen to pay the exorbitant fees to fast track my passport application process at that late date, my travel documents would not have arrived in time.

God exhorts us to keep our ears attentive to His voice and to be quick in our obedient response to that voice. Much like the unwise virgins in Matthew 25:1-13, I did not have oil in my lamp, and I missed a blessing as a result.

I know God forgave me, and I eventually forgave myself for my folly. Knowing God to be a loving God of second chances, I started the process of obtaining my passport the next week. A year later, I was blessed to take an extended road trip with two friends, and I cheerfully smiled as I presented my passport at the border crossing.

Perhaps you feel a nudge in your spirit to take care of some things that you have been putting off. Perhaps there are bills that need paying, perhaps your haven't changed the oil in your car for months, perhaps there is an awkward phone call that you need to make. Perhaps there is a neighbour that God has asked you to visit, and you've been dismissing the idea as a passing fancy. I hope my little cautionary tale of woe might serve to spur you to obey those quiet, everyday nudges God sends your way.

## Don't Let Your Light Diminish

Scented oil lamps were all the rage when I was a teen. I saved my babysitting money and by the end of the craze, I had three cute little lamps to my name. When the creative urge would rise, I would set up camp on my bedroom floor, sitting cross-legged with a hard pillow acting as my writing platform. Basking in the warm glow of lamplight, I would settle in for a quiet evening's worth of writing.

It was a chore to wash the glass fixtures with warm soapy water after every use. Several weeks would go by before I would clean my lamps. After a good wash, I would admire my handiwork and promise myself to keep the glass clean. The sparkling lampshade made it so I only required one lamp. Its singular light filled my little nook. With each consecutive use, the grime increased; oily soot from the previous use left a sticky residue that diminished the lamp's ability to cast light. As the weeks progressed, I needed to light one more lamp, then a third. It was only after my eyes began to water and I found it difficult to see through the stinky, hazy smoke caused by the dirty flues of my collective lamps that I would wash the glass chimneys. As I polished them with a soft cloth until they shone, I vowed to keep them clean. That promise was quickly forgotten as new ideas hurried across my brain all scrambling to get onto paper.

Jesus declares that we are the light of the world and encourages us to let our lights shine so to give glory to our heavenly Father. Much like my little lamps, our capacity to broadcast His light within us diminishes from the soot and grime that clings to us by living in a sinful world.

Matthew 5:14-16 - *"You are the light of the world. A city set on a hill cannot be hidden. Nor do people light a lamp and put it under a basket, but on a stand, and it gives light to all in the house. In the same way, let your light shine before others, so that they may see your good works and give glory to your Father who is in heaven"*

If we hide our light through compromise and inattentiveness, our flame become feeble. They produce little warmth, and they provide little illumination. Soot and grease eventually clog all ventilation holes, preventing the oxygen of the wind of the Spirit from flowing in and giving life to our flame.

John 17:15-18 - *"I do not ask that you take them out of the world, but that you keep them from the evil one. They are not of the world, just as I am not of the world. Sanctify them in the truth; your word is truth. As you sent me into the world, so I have sent them into the world."*

We serve a God who demonstrated His willingness to wash away the grit and grime of everyday life through Jesus' simple act of washing dusty feet. We serve a forgiving God who invites each of us to have our body, soul and spirit washed by His shed blood.

Ephesians 5:25-27 - *"Christ loved the church and gave himself up for her, that he might sanctify her, having cleansed her by the washing of water with the word, so that he might present the church to himself in splendor, without spot or wrinkle or any such thing, that she might be holy and without blemish."*

Take advantage of God's invitation and allow His cleansing waters to wash over you so that your earthly vessel may be an effective reflector of His light to the world.

## STONES OF REMEMBRANCE

Joshua 4:4-7 – *"Joshua called the twelve men from the people of Israel, whom he had appointed, a man from each tribe. And Joshua said to them, "Pass on before the ark of the Lord your God into the midst of the Jordan, and take up each of you a stone upon his shoulder, according to the number of the tribes of the people of Israel, that this may be a sign among you. When your children ask in time to come, 'What do those stones mean to you?' then you shall tell them that the waters of the Jordan were cut off before the ark of the covenant of the Lord. When it passed over the Jordan, the waters of the Jordan were cut off. So these stones shall be to the people of Israel a memorial forever."*

A spectacular view of a Tolkienian fantastical paradise as I traveled with companions on a day excursion in Thailand....

The warm, loving brown eyes of a brother in Christ as we bid each other farewell, knowing we would probably never see each other again, yet knowing we had a bond that crossed language and cultural barriers....

The deep, reassuring presence of God overwhelming me and

quieting my fears in a time of great stress....

A private Easter sunrise service attended only by myself and two friends as we danced on top of a hill, unable to contain the spontaneous joy and gratitude of the promise of new life....

The soft caress of a loving elderly aunt's hand on my cheek....

These memories are etched in my heart as I intentionally took it upon myself to never forget these precious gifts. I lay my stones of remembrance here.

I resolve to be alert to every blessing God brings my way and to live my life with purposeful gratitude. I resolve to live in the awareness that God continues to bless, instruct, and guide me even during times of darkness and deep personal struggle. I resolve to set within my spirit stones of remembrance so that no blessing, lesson, and life experience the Lord sends my way slips into the dusty confines of inattentiveness.

## *Peace! Be Still!*

As a child, I adored all storms: thunderstorms, blizzards, wind, rain, and hail. The wilder the weather, the more excited I would become. My parents placed locks high up on the screen doors to keep me inside because I would try to escape, longing to be one with the elements. There is still much of that child within me. A thunderstorm will find me with my nose plastered against my window as I watch lightning shoot across the sky. Walking against the wind with my cane is a challenge, but it's a challenge I embrace. I've been known to head out in the middle of a snowstorm to fetch a litre of milk.

However, even I have my limits. In July of 1987, I witnessed the destructive and terrifying power of a tornado that blew through my city. Several lives were lost, and there were dozens of people severely injured. The storm destroyed businesses and homes. Miraculously, the storm spared several oil refineries that flank the eastern border of the city. Many of my friends barely escaped with their lives as the tornado touched down during afternoon rush hour.

I huddled in the only windowless room in my basement

apartment. The thrills that went up and down my spine were not ones of exhilaration. I was terrified! Tornadoes are extremely rare in my region, and there was nothing familiar in the alien skies. The fierce winds and strange cloud formations had not been seen before; I was not prepared, and I was helpless.

Without warning, chaos hits our families, our workplaces, and our community. Unemployment hits; good kids are in trouble with the law; a severe illness or sudden death strikes. Domestic acts of terrorism bring home the horrors of war. Heartbreaking truths come to the light. Hidden sin is exposed, threatening to tear a church apart. We are caught in the vortex, tossed like rag dolls, bruised and tattered by the emotional debris that threatens to rip apart our heart.

What can one do when faced with such calamity? As Christ-followers, we have a safe refuge; as children of the Lord of the heavens, we can cry out for His mercy, grace, and strength. He who calmed the sea is the One who commanded order from chaos. (Genesis 1:2) We do not need to dwell on the fear of uncertainties, for we live on the right side of the cross. The cross assures us of His great love and provision for us. He will calm the seas in our lives; He will bring the emotional chaos to a place of peace. Although the physical storms of our lives may still rage around us, we can be at peace in the eye of the storm, safe from harm as we keep our eyes fixed on the Lord of all creation.

Lord Jesus, calm the storms of our hearts; keep us within Your peace as the circumstances of our world rage against us. We trust You; we know that You are our Redeemer, Saviour and Strong Tower. In times of trouble, our hearts will heed Your command, "Peace, be still."

## *I Don't Have to Always Know*

I have come to the freeing and exhilarating conclusion that I don't need to know all the answers to be a beloved child of God. It's not that I don't want to be knowledgeable about all the workings of the Kingdom. If anything, my longing to know God's heart grows stronger year by year. The Lord draws me to learn more about Him and His ways through pursuing deeper intimacy with Him. He encourages me to keep a teachable heart so I can recognize those He sends along my way as His messengers of truth and knowledge. However, all the important questions of life are answered at the foot of the cross.

Although I might have a slightly higher IQ than some, I realized long ago that knowledge and wisdom are not synonymous. I am disinterested in becoming a spiritual Jeopardy Champion.'I'll allow those with dizzying intellects, ready tongues, and quick wit to dazzle the rest of us. I'll applaud them as they come forward with just the right answer, said with the right attitude at just the perfect time.

Don't get me wrong; I delight as I sit at the feet of great teachers. I giggle with glee over newly gained insight as much as I rejoice in finding forgotten money in a jacket pocket. Although I freely admit to others that I don't have all the answers, I'm not content to stay in ignorance. I have free access to the One who holds all wisdom. God's Word reassures me that if I remain in a posture of humble respect, awe and deference toward the Lord, I will gain access to His true wisdom. Humble beginnings usually result in the best endings in the kingdom of God.

## Use Your Tools Wisely

In the late eighties, I was introduced to the potential of the Internet while working with Youth with A Mission. We communicated through simple electronic bulletin boards, discussion forums, and email. Missionaries and parachurch organizations marvelled as the world became a much smaller place. Outreaches that once took months to organize could now be arranged in weeks. Emergency prayer requests reached thousands of prayer warriors immediately. It was a time of great wonder, and we praised God for this exciting tool.

I received my first personal computer and home Internet access in 1993. After a few months of lurking in various groups, I dipped my toes into the water. I discovered that the Internet was full of supportive, caring individuals who were eager to help others. I joined a few interest groups, and I tried my hand at electronic evangelism. It was a heady time.

Even in those early years, I became aware of a major drawback to electronic communication. There was, and there still is, little consequence for one's actions beyond being banned from chat rooms for inappropriate behaviour. It was easy for misguided individuals to harass forums. Individuals deliberately joined Christian discussion boards to plant misinformation, rumours, and suspicion. Those of us who were more mature realized these troubled individuals were not necessarily evil; they were only looking for attention.

Many Christians fed the fires by glibly believing everything that was posted. They would then share these rumours and warnings without checking the facts for themselves. With the invention of search engines and myth-busting sites, Internet users today have no excuse, beyond pure laziness, for passing on misinformation.

I have watched Christians slander other believers, churches, and missionary organizations through innuendos and quotes taken out of context. Pastors preach on the destructive power of gossip from the pulpit on Sunday and blog scathing exposés of their rival's theological stances on Monday.

Although some pastors retract statements when they realize their mistake, the damage is already done. Unfortunately, readers are more drawn to a scathing denouncement of a public figure than a retraction of that denouncement. Once a search engine discovers an article on the Internet, it is nearly impossible to erase the damage done.

Christ's followers must be discerning and wise as when they read blogs, Facebook statuses and tweets. Think twice before passing on negative articles about ministries, pastors, and Christian public figures. It is our responsibility as Internet citizens to ask those who post scathing derogatory blogs to explain how and why they reached their conclusions. Where did they find their information?

Unfortunately, many exposés of denominational movements now line the aisles of Christian bookshelves. Many of those books are based purely on sound bites taken out of context, speculation, and second-hand information. Many of these authors made no attempt to speak to the party they felt they must expose. Some of the so-called facts these authors presented were based on hearsay and misquotes from old web articles. Although we now live in the electronic age, we are still bound to the command Jesus gave us 2,000 years ago.

Matthew 18:15 - *"If your brother sins against you, go and tell him his fault, between you and him alone. If he listens to you, you have gained your brother. But if he does not listen, take one or two others along with you, that every charge may be established by the evidence of two or three witnesses. If he refuses to listen to them, tell it to the church. And if he refuses to listen even to the church, let him be to you as a*

*Gentile and a tax collector."*

I am suspicious of individuals who refuse to state that they attempted to apply the Biblical principles of reconciliation, confrontation, and church discipline before the publication of their damning report.

I use Philippians 4:8-9 as a plumbline for every article I write and every quote that I use, and when I fail, I am quick to repent.

*"Finally, brothers, whatever is true, whatever is honourable, whatever is just, whatever is pure, whatever is lovely, whatever is commendable, if there is any excellence, if there is anything worthy of praise, think about these things. What you have learned and received and heard and seen in me—practice these things, and the God of peace will be with you."*

## *I'm Just Not That Strong*

Some Christians feel that they have no need for fellowship with other believers. Perhaps they are stronger than me. Perhaps they have developed a unique relationship with Jesus that is far superior to my own.

Kudos go to them! I am just not that strong. I need my brothers and sisters in Christ to support me, to pray for me and to challenge me as we grow in faith together, day-by-day, Sunday-by-Sunday, year-by-year. I need to be held accountable by those whom I have given permission to confront me when my faith walk and faith talk are not in synch.

My brothers and sisters in Christ rub me the wrong way at times, but if the truth were told, their rough edges rub against my rough edges the right way. My reactions to their imperfections expose character flaws and weaknesses that would remain hidden apart from face-to-face fellowship. I need my brothers and sisters. They remind me that life is not always about me. When there is more than just me around, I have to wait my turn. Sometimes, I need to be the one who sits in the audience and applauds the accomplishments of others.

God gave me arms to give and receive life-affirming hugs. He gave me hands to serve others; He gave me eyes to see the faces of those who need me as much as I need them. I guess I will never be a super saint that doesn't need the rest of the body.

Don't get me wrong. Jesus is my all-sufficiency. However, I believe He wouldn't have given His disciples the following command if He didn't think we needed each other as well.

John 13:34-35 - *"A new commandment I give to you, that you love one another: just as I have loved you, you also are to love one another. By this all people will know that you are my disciples, if you have love for one another."*

How can you One-Another by yourself?

## GOD OF ALL COMFORT

Inconsolable grief. The dictionary defines it as: sad beyond comforting; incapable of being consoled. Most of us have experienced such pain in our lives or have witnessed it in the lives of our friends and family.

It's heart-wrenching to bear witness to inconsolable grief. You want to take the pain away; you want to apply a magic salve that takes away the grievous injury. You long to speak the words that immediately stop the anguish; you want to speak the words that answer all the questions. You want to speak the words that soothe the spirit. You would do anything, you would go anywhere, and you would say anything, if only you could take them out of that unbearable pain, if even for a moment.

When I struggle to say just the right word or do the right thing, the Lord reminds me of just what my friends need me to be during such times of loss. They don't need my answers. They don't need my wisdom. They don't need a plan; they don't need a theological discourse on why there is evil in the world. Even the gentlest of words spoken at the wrong moment can assault the ears and bruise a wounded heart. What they need from me is for me to be me. They only need me to be there with them, and to stay present in their pain.

I remember the reception that followed my brother's funeral. Jim was one of my closest friends, my greatest cheerleader and my protector. My parent's house was swamped that afternoon; over 200 people were crammed in every nook and cranny of the split-level home. People from all walks of life were there, relatives, neighbours, old family friends, church members and high school buddies. All were there to bring comfort and to be comforted. I was exhausted, having travelled from Ontario to Calgary for the funeral. I had little sleep since his death, five days prior. I was still in shock and words of condolence washed over me like water.

Some younger people were there, most of who had not attended a funeral before. In their discomfort, they were speechless. One young girl I knew from a coffee house ministry solemnly charged me to remember Paul's exhortation, to rejoice in the Lord always. She suggested that I was sinning if I could not enjoy the fact that my brother was in heaven. At that moment, I just wanted my big brother's arm around my shoulders and to hear one of his corny puns. It was Jim's way to diffuse tension.

I managed to murmur a few kind words in response and

disappeared into the kitchen, looking for a quiet nook to be alone, even for a moment. Every chair was taken and so I leaned against the sink near the open window, hoping to catch a stray breeze. Immediately an elder from my brother's home church came along, wanting to know all about my missionary work. I know he had the best of intentions, but I politely excused myself after a vague answer. Elbowing my way through the hallway, I slipped out of the house and out onto my parent's front yard.

As it was a cold April day in Alberta, I shivered as I took a few cleansing breaths. Looking skyward, I sent a silent plea to the Lord, yearning for something, something that I couldn't put into words. Suddenly, I heard my name, and I turned around to find a dear friend standing there. Not a word was said as I was quickly enfolded in her arms. Another friend came alongside her to shelter us from prying eyes.

My pain was too deep for words and too deep for tears, but that hug gave me what I needed at that moment - the freedom to just be me in my grief. All I could say was, "I hurt." They held me a while longer. Through their hugs, I received a divine infusion of love and grace that upheld me and gave me the strength to be a support to my parents until it was time for me to leave again.

If someone in your life is hurting, I encourage you to be present for him or her. Stay still and listen, even when their pain is too deep for words or tears. It takes courage to stay present as you witness such pain. It takes discipline to resist giving into your desire to fix things as you watch a loved one suffer, but they need you to allow them to remain in their grief. It takes an enormous amount of trust in the God of all compassion but if you wait for His prompting, an apt word given at the right moment will become a conduit of immense healing and comfort.

Speak to the storm of your own heart, "Peace, be still" and you will carry that peace with you as a healing agent. Ask the Lord to comfort your own heart so you can draw from His well, and pour His comfort into those who grieve.

2 Corinthians 2: 3-5 - *"Blessed be the God and Father of our Lord Jesus Christ, the Father of mercies and God of all comfort, who comforts us in all our affliction, so that we may be able to comfort those who are in any affliction, with the comfort with which we ourselves are comforted by God. For as we share abundantly in Christ's sufferings, so through Christ we share abundantly in comfort too."*

## *The Wise Remain Students*

Proverbs 9:9 - "*Give instruction to a wise man, and he will be still wiser; teach a righteous man, and he will increase in learning.*"

The wisest people I know are the ones who have learned the art of listening, actually listening to those around them. Without a shred of prejudice and preconceived notions, the wise enter into every moment of their day with the attentive ear of a student.

The teacher of the day might be the multi-pierced supermarket clerk who demonstrates patience as the elderly gentleman at the front of the growing queue shakily counts out his pennies to make exact change. Perhaps the instructor comes as a two-year-old who points out the beauty and wonder of each and every stone along their daily walk. The lesson of the day might consist of hard questions asked by a heartbroken parent who struggles with the sudden loss of their beloved child. These sort of issues draw people, if they are wise, to admit their ineptness. They cause the spiritually wise to fall to their knees as they seek counsel from the Greatest Teacher of All.

Father God, keep us humble. Give us eyes to see and ears to

hear the teachers you belong our way. We acknowledge that we need to be discerning and weigh all things according to your Word, and yet we eagerly step into your School of Life. Amen.

## BLESSED ASSURANCE

If I could only use two words to describe what was impact Easter has had on my life, they would be "Blessed Assurance." I am profoundly grateful for the wondrous work of the cross, and the victory won on Resurrection Sunday.

Although I rejoice in song and worship along with my church family every Easter, the joy I feel goes so deep that I could not express it in words. I want to sit in silence and inhale the moment and yet; I want to shout out my triumphant joy in the same breath.

Have you ever won a desperate battle, a prolonged battle that required all your strength and faith, a battle that you were not sure of the outcome, and yet you continued to war? When the victory was finally won, and the initial adrenaline fueled elation faded, did you experience a quiet, profound peace? This blessed assurance rests in our hearts long after Easter has passed. As we face new battles that await us just beyond the horizon, this blessed assurance will carry us through as we keep our eyes focused on the prize already won!

1 Corinthians 15:55-58 - *"O death, where is your victory? O death, where is your sting?" The sting of death is sin, and the power of sin is the law. But thanks be to God, who gives us the victory through our Lord Jesus Christ. Therefore, my beloved brothers, be steadfast, immovable, always abounding in the work of the Lord, knowing that in the Lord your labor is not in vain."*

## Worship With No Agenda

Every summer, Canadians take advantage of the mild conditions and head for the highway. As a result, churches see a decline in their regular membership attendance and an increase in visitors. My church is no exception. One sunny Sunday, a close friend brought three visitors to church with her: an old friend who had suffered a recent stroke, a sister heavily involved in Eastern religions, and a niece who had not been in church for years.

My friend enters into deep communion with God during worship. She is not one to sit still. As the Spirit moves her, she kneels, raises her hands, or stands in quiet adoration. Being a natural-born worrier and knowing that my friend hoped her guests would come to know Jesus, I was concerned that her guests might be offended by the exuberance of our worship. Every song sung that morning focused on God's sovereignty, the blood of the Lamb and salvation. Every song in the worship set directly challenged the beliefs of my friend's pagan sister.

My friend didn't hold back that morning. She made no excuses for her passion, yet there was nothing in her stance that gave any indication that she was trying to make a point to anyone. She just wanted to bring pleasure to her King. While she honoured her guests, she honoured the heart of her Saviour even more.

God calls us to worship Him in spirit and truth. While worship is often a corporate experience, it must come from our individual expression of devotion blending with others, culminating in a harmonious chorus of praise. As long as our hearts remain centred on pleasing the Lord with our praise offering, the Lord will watch over those who we fear might be offended by our expression of worship.

When worship becomes a vehicle to make a point to those who serve other gods, then our worship is in vain. When we try to impress upon them that our God is bigger than their god, our focus becomes centred on something other than the person we came to worship. It is not pleasing to the Lord and such behaviour does not draw anyone to the Lord.

Worship expressed through the heart of devotion not only pleases God, but it also invites others to enter into a relationship with the One we worship.

Psalm 34:8 - *"Oh, taste and see that the Lord is good!"*

## *My Prayer For You*

I pray for peace.
Peace that passes all understanding.
Peace that fills every corner of your home,
Every corner of your heart,
Every corner of your life.

I pray for comfort.
Comfort that comes through the assurance
Of God's great love for you.
No matter what, no matter when, no matter why
No matter what you have done or will do,
His love will always be there.

I pray for the gift of earthly hands, feet, and voices that bring tangible evidence of His great love in practical ways.

I pray for grace to see your world through Christ's eyes.

## About the Author

Katherine's life is found in Christ, and so His name is sprinkled throughout her writings. You'll also find humour, wisdom and encouragement sprinkled in her writing as well! Although Katherine is physically disabled, she lives an active, productive life. After working with Youth With A Mission for 14 years, she eventually settled in Alberta Canada.

Katherine now oversees I Lift My Eyes Ministries, founded in 1995, reaching thousands across the Internet on a daily basis. Through her blog, mailing lists and impacting Social Media presence, Katherine's taking Christ's promise of an abundant, joy fueled life and running with it!

"Dare to Call Him Friend", Katherine's second book, is available to purchase on Kindle, Amazon, and her website, katherinewalden.com/dare

If you enjoyed this book, it would make the author's day if you would take a couple of minutes to leave a review at Amazon or Goodreads.com. Reviews are gold to an independent author.

## SPECIAL THANKS

How can I say thanks to my Harvest Vineyard Christian Fellowship family for your prayer support, your encouragement, your inspiration, and most of all, your love? You pushed me over the chicken line and into the realm of dreams come true.

My sincere gratitude goes to Lisa Thompson and Betty Rowe for your expertise and editorial assistance.

A special thanks to Alice Briggs of alicearlene.com for the wonderful cover graphics!

www.ingramcontent.com/pod-product-compliance
Lightning Source LLC
Chambersburg PA
CBHW061318040426
42444CB00011B/2696